Early in his career, **George Bernard Shaw** (1856–1950) wrote for newspapers and magazines as a critic of art, literature, music, and drama. From 1893 to 1939, the most active period of his career, Shaw wrote forty-seven plays. By 1915, his international fame was firmly established and productions of *Candida, Man and Superman, Arms and the Man,* and *The Devil's Disciple* appeared in many countries around the world. He went on to write such dramas as *Heartbreak House, Back to Methuselah, Androcles and the Lion,* and *Saint Joan.* Shaw is the only person to have won the Nobel Prize for Literature and an Oscar.

With the composer Frederick Loewe, **Alan Jay Lerner** (1918–86) created such classic musicals as *Brigadoon, Gigi, Camelot,* and *My Fair Lady.* Among his other collaborators were Kurt Weill (*Love Life*), Burton Lane (*Royal Wedding, On a Clear Day You Can See Forever*), Andre Previn (*Coco*), and Leonard Bernstein (*1600 Pennsylvania Avenue*). For his work, Lerner won several Oscars and a Grammy Award.

PYGMALION

A Romance in Five Acts

George Bernard Shaw

❧ AND ❧

MY FAIR LADY

Based on Shaw's *Pygmalion*

Adaptation and Lyrics by Alan Jay Lerner
Music by Frederick Loewe

SIGNET CLASSICS

SIGNET CLASSICS
Published by New American Library, a division of
Penguin Group (USA) Inc., 375 Hudson Street,
New York, New York 10014, USA
Penguin Group (Canada), 90 Eglinton Avenue East, Suite 700, Toronto,
Ontario M4P 2Y3, Canada (a division of Pearson Penguin Canada Inc.)
Penguin Books Ltd., 80 Strand, London WC2R 0RL, England
Penguin Ireland, 25 St. Stephen's Green, Dublin 2,
Ireland (a division of Penguin Books Ltd.)
Penguin Group (Australia), 250 Camberwell Road, Camberwell, Victoria 3124,
Australia (a division of Pearson Australia Group Pty. Ltd.)
Penguin Books India Pvt. Ltd., 11 Community Centre, Panchsheel Park,
New Delhi - 110 017, India
Penguin Group (NZ), cnr Airborne and Rosedale Roads, Albany,
Auckland 1310, New Zealand (a division of Pearson New Zealand Ltd.)
Penguin Books (South Africa) (Pty.) Ltd., 24 Sturdee Avenue,
Rosebank, Johannesburg 2196, South Africa

Penguin Books Ltd., Registered Offices:
80 Strand, London WC2R 0RL, England

Published by Signet Classics, an imprint of New American Library, a division
of Penguin Group (USA) Inc. This is an authorized paperback edition published by cooperation of the Society of Authors, London, England, and Alan
Jay Lerner.

First Signet Classics Printing, August 1980
20 19 18 17 16 15 14 13

Introduction copyright © Richard H. Goldstone, 1969
All rights reserved

(*For copyright information and permissions, see page 221.*)

℗ REGISTERED TRADEMARK—MARCA REGISTRADA

Printed in the United States of America

Contents

Introduction*

Pygmalion, possibly because it is Bernard Shaw's most overwhelmingly popular success, is the most underrated of his plays. In its first English production, it triumphantly starred the celebrated actress Mrs. Patrick Campbell. A generation later it was transformed, with additional material by Shaw, into a classic film with Wendy Hiller and the late Leslie Howard. Finally came its most extraordinary incarnation as *My Fair Lady*, originally produced with Rex Harrison and Julie Andrews. *My Fair Lady*, both as a staged musical comedy and subsequently as a film, has had the effect of eclipsing Shaw's play. The musical version of *Pygmalion*, with its appealing score and its colorful evocation of the period, is not the play that Shaw wrote; *My Fair Lady* simplifies one of Shaw's most fully and successfully realized stage works.

George Bernard Shaw composed his plays, usually, in the framework of one or another of his intellectual-political-economic-philosophical ideas: e.g., the technique of successful government (*Caesar and Cleopatra*); the evolutionary development of man's intellectual and physical capacities (*Man and Superman*); munitions making and the capitalist system (*Major Barbara*); the artist's role in society (*The Doctor's Dilemma*); world war and the problem of nationalism (*Heartbreak House*); tradition and change in collision (*Saint Joan*).

Pygmalion, by contrast, seems to be merely the portrayal of the involvement of three men with a girl (though Shaw wrote a long preface explaining that his play is really about phonetics. Later he wrote an afterword asserting that Eliza

*From the introduction to *Mentor Masterworks of Modern Drama*, Richard H. Goldstone, ed. (New York: New American Library, 1969)

ultimately married Freddy; and, reverting to his early career as a novelist, Shaw constructs an elaborate summary of Eliza and Freddy's life together as man and wife.) Shaw's disclaimers to the contrary, we are confronted by the fascinating dramatic situation that arises when a Pygmalion creates a Galatea; it is precisely the element that Shaw in his afterword attempts to deflect our attention from, which makes the play one of his artistically most satisfying: those emotional currents generated in a student-teacher relationship when the teacher is suffering from emotional malnutrition and the student is an attractive young woman.

Shaw regarded himself as a teacher and he regarded his plays as a means by which he might educate his generation. He despised most of the dramatic work of his time because the bulk of it was either melodrama or drawing room comedy. He even deplored what he regarded as the moral purposelessness of Shakespeare; plays about love affairs, Shaw contended in his preface to *Caesar and Cleopatra*, were not worthy of the attention of serious, mature people. But *Pygmalion* is a play about people in love, and what is more, it is one of the few plays by Shaw that reveal something of his deeply personal feelings. In his late fifties when he wrote *Pygmalion*, Shaw had become infatuated with the beautiful and fascinating Mrs. Campbell. Mrs. Campbell, though she welcomed the attentions of a distinguished and brilliant playwright and critic, allowing herself to become intimately involved with Shaw, was not in love with him and ultimately rejected his ardent advances to marry a younger man. Shaw's passion, his frustration, and the wound to his amour propre all spill over into the play, which appropriately opened in London (1914)—as Shaw had envisaged it in his writing of the play—with Mrs. Campbell in the role of Eliza. A record of the stormy correspondence between the playwright and the actress remains; as we read the letters we hear echoes of the play—with an important exception. In the play, the man retains his mastery of the situation.

My Fair Lady simplifies and conventionalizes the tortured relationship between the two principals. The requirements of a musical comedy result in the music and lyrics displacing half the dialogue of the play. Liza and Henry Higgins of the musical, consequently, lose some of their individuality, some of their humanity. Liza becomes Cinderella and Higgins is transformed into a slightly crusty prince. Shaw maintained in his afterword that Higgins and Liza never marry each other because they both realize that they would make each other miserable. No reservation of that kind would occur to the audiences of the musical version. In *My Fair Lady* there is an unambiguously happy ending: Shaw's ending is deliberately inconclusive. What we know when the curtain comes down is that Liza and Higgins have finally come to terms with their mutual need. And that is resolution enough . . . enough for Shaw, and enough for us, once we have become reconciled to the idea that in art, just as in life, we cannot expect unqualifiedly happy endings.

Pygmalion is one of Shaw's least didactic plays; but that is not to say that Shaw had eliminated his characteristically incisive social analysis. England in the early decades of the twentieth century was obsessed by the matter of class status, by the gradations of the rigid social structure. The upper middle class—that is to say, Britain's *ladies* and *gentlemen*—achieved their precious status through the fortuitous combination of birth, education, profession (if any), and manner of dress. Money was normally a prerequisite to status, but one could struggle along without very much of it if one belonged to the right family.

Shaw observes in *Pygmalion* that the right accent (together with the right clothes) could carry the day. His position in relation to class was not that society should eliminate the concept of *ladies* and *gentlemen* but that the status of lady or gentleman might be attained by anyone with intelligence and character who aspired to the part. Shaw makes clear that class distinctions lose their force when a decent education can transform a street vendor into a "duchess"; that education made available to all those with the intellectual means of profiting from it would eliminate the outworn concepts of caste and class.

—Richard H. Goldstone

George Bernard Shaw: *Pygmalion*

*George Bernard Shaw (1856–1950) was born in Ireland
and moved to England while he was still in his teens. In
his twenties Shaw divided his time between writing unsuccessful novels and observing the wretched conditions of
the London poor. In his thirties Shaw established himself
as a critic of art, music, and drama. His career as a playwright coincided with the onset of middle age. His slow
metamorphosis from an unknown, unsuccessful novelist
to the best-known writer of his time has been the subject
of a number of books, the best of which is St. John Er-
vine's* Bernard Shaw. *His most representative plays are:*
Mrs. Warren's Profession *(1893),* Arms and the Man
(1894), Candida *(1894),* The Devil's Disciple *(1896),*
Caesar and Cleopatra *(1899),* Man and Superman
(1903), Major Barbara *(1905),* The Doctor's Dilemma
(1906), Heartbreak House *(1920),* Saint Joan *(1924),* The
Apple Cart *(1929), and* Too True to be Good *(1932).*

Bernard Shaw wrote in a 1942 preface to *Pygmalion*
(1913) "that it is impossible for an Englishman to open
his mouth without making some other Englishman despise him." In England (and even, to a certain extent,
in the United States) speech is perhaps the most important clue in determining caste or class. *Pygmalion* has as
its subject-theme the institutions man has constructed to
help perpetuate both the privileges of the rich and the
servility of the poor.

The passionate sincerity and the desperate earnestness
that lie behind the surface play of Shaw's most successful

comedy have as their origin the fact that Shaw spent the best part of his youth, the decade of his twenties, tramping the streets of London observing the extremes of wealth and poverty. Shocked by what he saw, he became a founding member of the Fabian Society, a political group committed to Socialism, the progenitor of Britain's Labour Party.

Shaw's earliest plays explicitly dealt with economic and social injustice. Sober, earnest, old-fashioned, they were failures. Not until Shaw found his own voice—in plays comically saturated with paradox and irreverence, a genre now known as Shavian comedy—did his impact on England and the world exceed that of any other playwright of the twentieth century.

What Shaw learned was that before he could persuade an audience to think, he must first provoke laughter—and then tears. At what point in the play do we become involved and indignant about the plight of Eliza Doolittle? Like her benefactors, we continue to regard her as something not unlike a trained dog—until the moment we realize that because of the accident of birth a young woman of character and intelligence has been condemned to a lifetime of squalor and hopelessness. Then, and only then, do we realize that Shaw has used his Cockney Cinderella as a symbol of the world's dispossessed whose hope lies in the availability of education and the good will of those more fortunate among us.

Publisher's Note

George Bernard Shaw, as is evident from the following quotation in *The Author* (April 1902), had some highly personal—and strongly held—opinions about spelling and punctuation:

> The apostrophes in ain't, don't, haven't, etc. look so ugly that the most careful printing cannot make a page of colloquial dialogue as handsome as a page of classical dialogue. Besides, shan't should be sha"n't, if the wretched pedantry of indicating the elision is to be carried out. I have written aint, dont, havnt, shant, shouldnt and wont for twenty years with perfect impunity, using the apostrophe only where its omission would suggest another word: for example, hell for he'll. There is not the faintest reason for persisting in the ugly and silly trick of peppering pages with these uncouth bacilli. I also write thats, whats, lets, for the colloquial forms of that is, what is, let us; and I have not yet been prosecuted.

This edition of *Pygmalion* follows Shaw's dictates in these matters.

PYGMALION

A Romance in Five Acts

by
George Bernard Shaw

Pygmalion

Composition begun 7 March 1912; completed early June 1912. First published in German translation, 1913. Published in *Everybody's Magazine* (New York), November 1914, and in *Nash's Magazine,* November–December 1914. First collected in *Androcles and the Lion, Overruled, Pygmalion,* 1916. Revised 1941 for separate printing of *Pygmalion* in Standard Edition text, also incorporating several revised sequences from the film scenario. This revision was followed for the Penguin Books edition later in 1941. First presented in German at the Hofburg Theater, Vienna, on 16 October 1913. First presented in English at His Majesty's Theatre, London, on 11 April 1914.

CLARA EYNSFORD-HILL, *Margaret Bussé*
MRS EYNSFORD-HILL, *Carlotta Addison*
A BYSTANDER, *Roy Byford*
FREDDY EYNSFORD-HILL, *Algernon Greig*
ELIZA DOOLITTLE, *Mrs Patrick Campbell*
COLONEL PICKERING, *Philip Merivale*
HENRY HIGGINS, *Herbert Tree*
A SARCASTIC BYSTANDER, *Alexander Sarner*
MRS PEARCE, *Geraldine Olliffe*
ALFRED DOOLITTLE, *Edmund Gurney*
MRS HIGGINS, *Rosamond Mayne-Young*
PARLORMAID, *Irene Delisse*

Period—The Present

ACT ONE *The Portico of St Paul's,*
Covent Garden 11:15 p.m.

ACT TWO *Professor Higgins's Phonetic Laboratory, Wim-*
pole Street. Next day. 11 a.m.

ACT THREE *The Drawing Room in Mrs Higgins's Flat on*
Chelsea Embankment. Several Months Later.
At-Home Day

ACT FOUR *The Same as Act 2. Several Months Later.*
Midnight

ACT FIVE *The Same as Act 3. The Following Morning*

NOTE FOR TECHNICIANS. A complete representation of the
play as printed for the first time in this edition is techni-
cally possible only on the cinema screen or on stages
furnished with exceptionally elaborate machinery. For
ordinary theatrical use the scenes separated by rows of
asterisks are to be omitted.

In the dialogue an e upside down indicates the indefi-
nite vowel, sometimes called obscure or neutral, for
which, though it is one of the commonest sounds in English speech, our wretched alphabet has no letter.

ACT ONE

London at 11:15 p.m. Torrents of heavy summer rain. Cab whistles blowing frantically in all directions. Pedestrians running for shelter into the portico of St Paul's church (not Wren's cathedral but Inigo Jones's church in Covent Garden vegetable market), among them a lady and her daughter in evening dress. All are peering out gloomily at the rain, except one man with his back turned to the rest, wholly preoccupied with a notebook in which he is writing.

The church clock strikes the first quarter.

THE DAUGHTER (*in the space between the central pillars, close to the one on her left*): I'm getting chilled to the bone. What can Freddy be doing all this time? He's been gone twenty minutes.

THE MOTHER (*on her daughter's right*): Not so long. But he ought to have got us a cab by this.

A BYSTANDER (*on the lady's right*): He wont get no cab not until half-past eleven, missus, when they come back after dropping their theatre fares.

THE MOTHER: But we must have a cab. We cant stand here until half-past eleven. It's too bad.

THE BYSTANDER: Well, it aint my fault, missus.

THE DAUGHTER: If Freddy had a bit of gumption, he would have got one at the theatre door.

THE MOTHER: What could he have done, poor boy?

THE DAUGHTER: Other people got cabs. Why couldnt he?

(*Freddy rushes in out of the rain from the Southampton*

5

*Street side, and comes between them closing a dripping
umbrella. He is a young man of twenty, in evening dress,
very wet round the ankles.*)

THE DAUGHTER: Well, havnt you got a cab?

FREDDY: Theres not one to be had for love or money.

THE MOTHER: Oh, Freddy, there must be one. You cant
have tried.

THE DAUGHTER: It's too tiresome. Do you expect us
to go and get one ourselves?

FREDDY: I tell you theyre all engaged. The rain was
so sudden: nobody was prepared; and everybody had to
take a cab. Ive been to Charing Cross one way and
nearly to Ludgate Circus the other; and they were all
engaged.

THE MOTHER: Did you try Trafalgar Square?

FREDDY: There wasnt one at Trafalgar Square.

THE DAUGHTER: Did you try?

FREDDY: I tried as far as Charing Cross Station. Did
you expect me to walk to Hammersmith?

THE DAUGHTER: You havnt tried at all.

THE MOTHER: You really are very helpless, Freddy. Go
again; and dont come back until you have found a cab.

FREDDY: I shall simply get soaked for nothing.

THE DAUGHTER: And what about us? Are we to stay
here all night in this draught, with next to nothing on?
You selfish pig—

FREDDY: Oh, very well: I'll go, I'll go. (*He opens his
umbrella and dashes off Strandwards, but comes into collision with a flower girl who is hurrying in for shelter,
knocking her basket out of her hands. A blinding flash of
lightning, followed instantly by a rattling peal of thunder,
orchestrates the incident.*)

THE FLOWER GIRL: Nah then, Freddy: look wh' y'
gowin, deah.

FREDDY: Sorry (*he rushes off*).

THE FLOWER GIRL (*picking up her scattered flowers and
replacing them in the basket*): Theres menners f' yer! Tə-
oo branches o voylets trod into the mad. (*She sits down
on the plinth of the column, sorting her flowers, on the*

lady's right. She is not at all a romantic figure. She is perhaps eighteen, perhaps twenty, hardly older. She wears a little sailor hat of black straw that has long been exposed to the dust and soot of London and has seldom if ever been brushed. Her hair needs washing rather badly: its mousy color can hardly be natural. She wears a shoddy black coat that reaches nearly to her knees and is shaped to her waist. She has a brown skirt with a coarse apron. Her boots are much the worse for wear. She is no doubt as clean as she can afford to be; but compared to the ladies she is very dirty. Her features are no worse than theirs; but their condition leaves something to be desired; and she needs the services of a dentist.)

THE MOTHER: How do you know that my son's name is Freddy, pray?

THE FLOWER GIRL: Ow, eez yə-ooa san, is e? Wal, fewd dan y' də-ooty bawmz a mather should, eed now bettern to spawl a pore gel's flahrzn than ran awy athaht pyin. Will ye-oo py me f'them? (*Here, with apologies, this desperate attempt to represent her dialect without a phonetic alphabet must be abandoned as unintelligible outside London.*)

THE DAUGHTER: Do nothing of the sort, mother. The idea!

THE MOTHER: Please allow me, Clara. Have you any pennies?

THE DAUGHTER: No. Ive nothing smaller than sixpence.

THE FLOWER GIRL (*hopefully*): I can give you change for a tanner, kind lady.

THE MOTHER (*to Clara*): Give it to me. (*Clara parts reluctantly.*) Now (*to the girl*). This is for your flowers.

THE FLOWER GIRL: Thank you kindly, lady.

THE DAUGHTER: Make her give you the change. These things are only a penny a bunch.

THE MOTHER: Do hold your tongue, Clara. (*To the girl*) You can keep the change.

THE FLOWER GIRL: Oh, thank you, lady.

THE MOTHER: Now tell me how you know that young gentleman's name.

THE FLOWER GIRL: I didnt.

THE MOTHER: I heard you call him by it. Dont try to deceive me.

THE FLOWER GIRL (*protesting*): Who's trying to deceive you? I called him Freddy or Charlie same as you might yourself if you was talking to a stranger and wished to be pleasant.

THE DAUGHTER: Sixpence thrown away! Really, mamma, you might have spared Freddy that. (*She retreats in disgust behind the pillar.*)

(*An elderly gentleman of the amiable military type rushes into the shelter, and closes a dripping umbrella. He is in the same plight as Freddy, very wet about the ankles. He is in evening dress, with a light overcoat. He takes the place left vacant by the daughter.*)

THE GENTLEMAN: Phew!

THE MOTHER (*to the gentleman*): Oh sir, is there any sign of its stopping?

THE GENTLEMAN: I'm afraid not. It started worse than ever about two minutes ago (*he goes to the plinth beside the flower girl; puts up his foot on it; and stoops to turn down his trouser ends*).

THE MOTHER: Oh dear! (*She retires sadly and joins her daughter.*)

THE FLOWER GIRL (*taking advantage of the military gentleman's proximity to establish friendly relations with him*): If it's worse, it's a sign it's nearly over. So cheer up, Captain; and buy a flower off a poor girl.

THE GENTLEMAN: I'm sorry. I havnt any change.

THE FLOWER GIRL: I can give you change, Captain.

THE GENTLEMAN: For a sovereign? Ive nothing less.

THE FLOWER GIRL: Garn! Oh do buy a flower off me, Captain. I can change half-a-crown. Take this for tuppence.

THE GENTLEMAN: Now dont be troublesome: theres a good girl. (*Trying his pockets*) I really havnt any change—Stop: heres three hapence, if thats any use to you (*he retreats to the other pillar*).

THE FLOWER GIRL (*disappointed, but thinking three halfpence better than nothing*): Thank you, sir.

THE BYSTANDER (*to the girl*): You be careful: give him a flower for it. Theres a bloke here behind taking down every blessed word youre saying. (*All turn to the man who is taking notes.*)

THE FLOWER GIRL (*springing up terrified*): I aint done nothing wrong by speaking to the gentleman. Ive a right to sell flowers if I keep off the kerb. (*Hysterically*) I'm a respectable girl: so help me, I never spoke to him except to ask him to buy a flower off me.

(*General hubbub, mostly sympathetic to the flower girl, but deprecating her excessive sensibility. Cries of* Dont start hollerin. Who's hurting you? Nobody's going to touch you. Whats the good of fussing? Steady on. Easy easy, *etc., come from the elderly staid spectators, who pat her comfortingly. Less patient ones bid her shut her head, or ask her roughly what is wrong with her. A remoter group, not knowing what the matter is, crowd in and increase the noise with question and answer:* Whats the row? What-she do? Where is he? A tec taking her down. What! him? Yes: him over there: Took money off the gentleman, *etc.*)

THE FLOWER GIRL (*breaking through them to the gentleman, crying wildly*): Oh, sir, dont let him charge me. You dunno what it means to me. Theyll take away my character and drive me on the streets for speaking to gentlemen. They—

THE NOTE TAKER (*coming forward on her right, the rest crowding after him*): There! there! there! there! who's hurting you, you silly girl? What do you take me for?

THE BYSTANDER: It's aw rawt: e's a gentleman: look at his bə-oots. (*Explaining to the note taker*) She thought you was a copper's nark, sir.

THE NOTE TAKER (*with quick interest*): Whats a copper's nark?

THE BYSTANDER (*inapt at definition*): It's a—well, it's a copper's nark, as you might say. What else would you call it? A sort of informer.

THE FLOWER GIRL (*still hysterical*): I take my Bible oath I never said a word—

THE NOTE TAKER (*overbearing but good-humored*): Oh, shut up, shut up. Do I look like a policeman?

THE FLOWER GIRL (*far from reassured*): Then what did you take down my words for? How do I know whether you took me down right? You just shew me what youve wrote about me. (*The note taker opens his book and holds it steadily under her nose though the pressure of the mob trying to read it over his shoulders would upset a weaker man.*) Whats that? That aint proper writing. I cant read that.

THE NOTE TAKER: I can. (*Reads, reproducing her pronunciation exactly*) "Cheer ap, Keptin; n' baw ya flahr orf a pore gel."

THE FLOWER GIRL (*much distressed*): It's because I called him Captain. I meant no harm. (*To the gentleman*) Oh, sir, dont let him lay a charge agen me for a word like that. You—

THE GENTLEMAN: Charge! I make no charge. (*To the note taker*) Really, sir, if you are a detective, you need not begin protecting me against molestation by young women until I ask you. Anybody could see that the girl meant no harm.

THE BYSTANDERS GENERALLY (*demonstrating against police espionage*): Course they could. What business is it of yours? You mind your own affairs. He wants promotion, he does. Taking down people's words! Girl never said a word to him. What harm if she did? Nice thing a girl cant shelter from the rain without being insulted, etc., etc., etc. (*She is conducted by the more sympathetic demonstrators back to her plinth, where she resumes her seat and struggles with her emotion.*)

THE BYSTANDER: He aint a tec. He's a blooming busybody: thats what he is. I tell you, look at his bo-oots.

THE NOTE TAKER (*turning on him genially*): And how are all your people down at Selsey?

THE BYSTANDER (*suspiciously*): Who told you my people come from Selsey?

THE NOTE TAKER: Never you mind. They did. (*To the girl*) How do you come to be up so far east? You were born in Lisson Grove.

THE FLOWER GIRL (*appalled*): Oh, what harm is there in my leaving Lisson Grove? It wasnt fit for a pig to live in; and I had to pay four-and-six a week. (*In tears*) Oh, boo—hoo—oo—

THE NOTE TAKER: Live where you like; but stop that noise.

THE GENTLEMAN (*to the girl*): Come, come! he cant touch you: you have a right to live where you please.

A SARCASTIC BYSTANDER (*thrusting himself between the note taker and the gentleman*): Park Lane, for instance. I'd like to go into the Housing Question with you, I would.

THE FLOWER GIRL (*subsiding into a brooding melancholy over her basket, and talking very low-spiritedly to herself*): I'm a good girl, I am.

THE SARCASTIC BYSTANDER (*not attending to her*): Do you know where *I* come from?

THE NOTE TAKER (*promptly*): Hoxton.

(*Titterings. Popular interest in the note taker's performance increases.*)

THE SARCASTIC ONE (*amazed*): Well, who said I didnt? Bly me! you know everything, you do.

THE FLOWER GIRL (*still nursing her sense of injury*): Aint no call to meddle with me, he aint.

THE BYSTANDER (*to her*): Of course he aint. Dont you stand it from him. (*To the note taker*) See here: what call have you to know about people what never offered to meddle with you?

THE FLOWER GIRL: Let him say what he likes. I dont want to have no truck with him.

THE BYSTANDER: You take us for dirt under your feet, dont you? Catch you taking liberties with a gentleman!

THE SARCASTIC BYSTANDER: Yes: tell him where he come from if you want to go fortune-telling.

THE NOTE TAKER: Cheltenham, Harrow, Cambridge, and India.

THE GENTLEMAN: Quite right.

(*Great laughter. Reaction in the note taker's favor. Exclamations of* He knows all about it. Told him proper. Hear him tell the toff where he come from? etc.)

THE GENTLEMAN: May I ask, sir, do you do this for your living at a music hall?

THE NOTE TAKER: Ive thought of that. Perhaps I shall some day.

(*The rain has stopped; and the persons on the outside of the crowd begin to drop off.*)

THE FLOWER GIRL (*resenting the reaction*): He's no gentleman, he aint, to interfere with a poor girl.

THE DAUGHTER (*out of patience, pushing her way rudely to the front and displacing the gentleman, who politely retires to the other side of the pillar*): What on earth is Freddy doing? I shall get pneumownia if I stay in this draught any longer.

THE NOTE TAKER (*to himself, hastily making a note of her pronunciation of "monia"*): Earlscourt.

THE DAUGHTER (*violently*): Will you please keep your impertinent remarks to yourself.

THE NOTE TAKER: Did I say that out loud? I didnt mean to. I beg your pardon. Your mother's Epsom, unmistakeably.

THE MOTHER (*advancing between her daughter and the note taker*): How very curious! I was brought up in Largelady Park, near Epsom.

THE NOTE TAKER (*uproariously amused*): Ha! ha! What a devil of a name! Excuse me. (*To the daughter*) You want a cab, do you?

THE DAUGHTER: Dont dare speak to me.

THE MOTHER: Oh please, please, Clara. (*Her daughter repudiates her with an angry shrug and retires haughtily.*) We should be so grateful to you, sir, if you found us a cab. (*The note taker produces a whistle.*) Oh, thank you. (*She joins her daughter.*)

(*The note taker blows a piercing blast.*)

THE SARCASTIC BYSTANDER: There! I knowed he was a plainclothes copper.

THE BYSTANDER: That aint a police whistle: thats a sporting whistle.

THE FLOWER GIRL (*still preoccupied with her wounded feelings*): He's no right to take away my character. My character is the same to me as any lady's.

THE NOTE TAKER: I dont know whether youve noticed it; but the rain stopped about two minutes ago.

THE BYSTANDER: So it has. Why didnt you say so before? and us losing our time listening to your silliness! (*He walks off towards the Strand.*)

THE SARCASTIC BYSTANDER: I can tell where you come from. You come from Anwell. Go back there.

THE NOTE TAKER (*helpfully*): *H*anwell.

THE SARCASTIC BYSTANDER (*affecting great distinction of speech*): Thenk you, teacher. Haw haw! So long (*he touches his hat with mock respect and strolls off*).

THE FLOWER GIRL: Frightening people like that! How would he like it himself?

THE MOTHER: It's quite fine now, Clara. We can walk to a motor bus. Come. (*She gathers her skirts above her ankles and hurries off towards the Strand.*)

THE DAUGHTER: But the cab—(*her mother is out of hearing*). Oh, how tiresome! (*She follows angrily.*)

(*All the rest have gone except the note taker, the gentleman, and the flower girl, who sits arranging her basket, and still pitying herself in murmurs.*)

THE FLOWER GIRL: Poor girl! Hard enough for her to live without being worrited and chivied.

THE GENTLEMAN (*returning to his former place on the note taker's left*): How do you do it, if I may ask?

THE NOTE TAKER: Simply phonetics. The science of speech. Thats my profession: also my hobby. Happy is the man who can make a living by his hobby! You can spot an Irishman or a Yorkshireman by his brogue. *I* can place any man within six miles. I can place him within two miles in London. Sometimes within two streets.

THE FLOWER GIRL: Ought to be ashamed of himself, unmanly coward!

THE GENTLEMAN: But is there a living in that?

THE NOTE TAKER: Oh yes. Quite a fat one. This is an age of upstarts. Men begin in Kentish Town with £80 a year, and end in Park Lane with a hundred thousand. They want to drop Kentish Town; but they give themselves away every time they open their mouths. Now I can teach them—

THE FLOWER GIRL: Let him mind his own business and leave a poor girl—

THE NOTE TAKER (*explosively*): Woman: cease this detestable boohooing instantly; or else seek the shelter of some other place of worship.

THE FLOWER GIRL (*with feeble defiance*): Ive a right to be here if I like, same as you.

THE NOTE TAKER: A woman who utters such depressing and disgusting sounds has no right to be anywhere—no right to live. Remember that you are a human being with a soul and the divine gift of articulate speech: that your native language is the language of Shakespear and Milton and The Bible; and dont sit there crooning like a bilious pigeon.

THE FLOWER GIRL (*quite overwhelmed, looking up at him in mingled wonder and deprecation without daring to raise her head*): Ah-ah-ah-ow-ow-ow-oo!

THE NOTE TAKER (*whipping out his book*): Heavens! what a sound! (*He writes; then holds out the book and reads, reproducing her vowels exactly*) Ah-ah-ah-ow-ow-ow-oo!

THE FLOWER GIRL (*tickled by the performance, and laughing in spite of herself*): Garn!

THE NOTE TAKER: You see this creature with her kerbstone English: the English that will keep her in the gutter to the end of her days. Well, sir, in three months I could pass that girl off as a duchess at an ambassador's garden party. I could even get her a place as lady's maid or shop assistant, which requires better English.

THE FLOWER GIRL: Whats that you say?

THE NOTE TAKER: Yes, you squashed cabbage leaf, you disgrace to the noble architecture of these columns, you incarnate insult to the English language: I could pass you off as the Queen of Sheba. (*To the gentleman*) Can you believe that?

THE GENTLEMAN: Of course I can. I am myself a student of Indian dialects; and—

THE NOTE TAKER (*eagerly*): Are you? Do you know Colonel Pickering, the author of Spoken Sanscrit?

THE GENTLEMAN: I am Colonel Pickering. Who are you?

THE NOTE TAKER: Henry Higgins, author of Higgins's Universal Alphabet.

PICKERING (*with enthusiasm*): I came from India to meet you.

HIGGINS: I was going to India to meet you.

PICKERING: Where do you live?

HIGGINS: 27A Wimpole Street. Come and see me tomorrow.

PICKERING: I'm at the Carlton. Come with me now and lets have a jaw over some supper.

HIGGINS: Right you are.

THE FLOWER GIRL (*to Pickering, as he passes her*): Buy a flower, kind gentleman. I'm short for my lodging.

PICKERING: I really havnt any change. I'm sorry (*he goes away*).

HIGGINS (*shocked at the girl's mendacity*): Liar. You said you could change half-a-crown.

THE FLOWER GIRL (*rising in desperation*): You ought to be stuffed with nails, you ought. (*Flinging the basket at his feet*) Take the whole blooming basket for sixpence.

(*The church clock strikes the second quarter.*)

HIGGINS (*hearing in it the voice of God, rebuking him for his Pharisaic want of charity to the poor girl*): A reminder. (*He raises his hat solemnly; then throws a handful of money into the basket and follows Pickering.*)

THE FLOWER GIRL (*picking up a half-crown*): Ah-ow-ooh! (*Picking up a couple of florins*) Aaaaah-ow-ooh! (*Picking up several coins*) Aaaaaaah-ow-ooh! (*Picking up a half-sovereign*) Aaaaaaaaaaaah-ow-ooh!!!

FREDDY (*springing out of a taxicab*): Got one at last.

Hallo! (*To the girl*) Where are the two ladies that were here?

THE FLOWER GIRL: They walked to the bus when the rain stopped.

FREDDY: And left me with a cab on my hands! Damnation!

THE FLOWER GIRL (*with grandeur*): Never mind, young man. I'm going home in a taxi. (*She sails off to the cab. The driver puts his hand behind him and holds the door firmly shut against her. Quite understanding his mistrust, she shews him her handful of money.*) A taxi fare aint no object to me, Charlie. (*He grins and opens the door.*) Here. What about the basket?

THE TAXIMAN: Give it here. Tuppence extra.

LIZA: No: I dont want nobody to see it. (*She crushes it into the cab and gets in, continuing the conversation through the window.*) Goodbye, Freddy.

FREDDY (*dazedly raising his hat*): Goodbye.

TAXIMAN: Where to?

LIZA: Bucknam Pellis [Buckingham Palace].

TAXIMAN: What d'ye mean—Bucknam Pellis?

LIZA: Dont you know where it is? In the Green Park, where the King lives. Goodbye, Freddy. Dont let me keep you standing there. Goodbye.

FREDDY: Goodbye. (*He goes.*)

TAXIMAN: Here? Whats this about Bucknam Pellis? What business have you at Bucknam Pellis?

LIZA: Of course I havnt none. But I wasnt going to let him know that. You drive me home.

TAXIMAN: And wheres home?

LIZA: Angel Court, Drury Lane, next Meiklejohn's oil shop.

TAXIMAN: That sounds more like it, Judy. (*He drives off.*)

*   *   *

Let us follow the taxi to the entrance to Angel Court, a narrow little archway between two shops, one of them

Meiklejohn's oil shop. When it stops there, Eliza gets out, dragging her basket with her.

LIZA: How much?

TAXIMAN (*indicating the taximeter*): Cant you read? A shilling.

LIZA: A shilling for two minutes!!

TAXIMAN: Two minutes or ten: it's all the same.

LIZA: Well, I dont call it right.

TAXIMAN: Ever been in a taxi before?

LIZA (*with dignity*): Hundreds and thousands of times, young man.

TAXIMAN (*laughing at her*): Good for you, Judy. Keep the shilling, darling, with best love from all at home. Good luck! (*He drives off.*)

LIZA (*humiliated*): Impidence!

(*She picks up the basket and trudges up the alley with it to her lodging: a small room with very old wall paper hanging loose in the damp places. A broken pane in the window is mended with paper. A portrait of a popular actor and a fashion plate of ladies' dresses, all wildly beyond poor Eliza's means, both torn from newspapers, are pinned up on the wall. A bird-cage hangs in the window; but its tenant died long ago: it remains as a memorial only.*

These are the only visible luxuries: the rest is the irreducible minimum of poverty's needs: a wretched bed heaped with all sorts of coverings that have any warmth in them, a draped packing case with a basin and jug on it and a little looking glass over it, a chair and table, the refuse of some suburban kitchen, and an American alarum clock on the shelf above the unused fireplace: the whole lighted with a gas lamp with a penny in the slot meter. Rent: four shillings a week.)

Here Eliza, chronically weary, but too excited to go to bed, sits, counting her new riches and dreaming and planning what to do with them, until the gas goes out, when she enjoys for the first time the sensation of being able to put in another penny without grudging it. This prodigal mood does not extinguish her gnawing sense of the need for economy sufficiently to prevent her from calculating that she can dream and plan in bed more cheaply and warmly than sitting up without a fire. So she takes off her shawl and skirt and adds them to the miscellaneous bedclothes. Then she kicks off her shoes and gets into bed without any further change.

ACT TWO

Next day at 11 a.m. Higgins's laboratory in Wimpole Street. It is a room on the first floor, looking on the street, and was meant for the drawing room. The double doors are in the middle of the back wall; and persons entering find in the corner to their right two tall file cabinets at right angles to one another against the walls. In this corner stands a flat writing-table, on which are a phonograph, a laryngoscope, a row of tiny organ pipes with a bellows, a set of lamp chimneys for singing flames with burners attached to a gas plug in the wall by an indiarubber tube, several tuning-forks of different sizes, a life-size image of half a human head, shewing in section the vocal organs, and a box containing a supply of wax cylinders for the phonograph.

Further down the room, on the same side, is a fireplace, with a comfortable leather-covered easy-chair at the side of the hearth nearest the door, and a coal-scuttle. There is a clock on the mantel-piece. Between the fireplace and the phonograph table is a stand for newspapers.

On the other side of the central door, to the left of the visitor, is a cabinet of shallow drawers. On it is a telephone and the telephone directory. The corner beyond, and most of the side wall, is occupied by a grand piano, with the keyboard at the end furthest from the door, and a bench for the player extending the full length of the keyboard. On the piano is a dessert dish heaped with fruit and sweets, mostly chocolates.

The middle of the room is clear. Besides the easy-chair, the piano bench, and two chairs at the phonograph table, *there is one stray chair. It stands near the fireplace. On the walls, engravings: mostly Piranesis and mezzotint portraits. No paintings.*

Pickering is seated at the table, putting down some cards and a tuning-fork which he has been using. Higgins is standing up near him, closing two or three file drawers which are hanging out. He appears in the morning light as a robust, vital, appetizing sort of man of forty or thereabouts, dressed in a professional-looking black frock-coat with a white linen collar and black silk tie. He is of the energetic, scientific type, heartily, even violently interested in everything that can be studied as a scientific subject, and careless about himself and other people, including their feelings. He is, in fact, but for his years and size, rather like a very impetuous baby "taking notice" eagerly and loudly, and requiring almost as much watching to keep him out of unintended mischief. His manner varies from genial bullying when he is in a good humor to stormy petulance when anything goes wrong; but he is so entirely frank and void of malice that he remains likeable even in his least reasonable moments.

HIGGINS (*as he shuts the last drawer*): Well, I think thats the whole show.

PICKERING: It's really amazing. I havnt taken half of it in, you know.

HIGGINS: Would you like to go over any of it again?

PICKERING (*rising and coming to the fireplace, where he plants himself with his back to the fire*): No, thank you: not now. I'm quite done up for this morning.

HIGGINS (*following him, and standing beside him on his left*): Tired of listening to sounds?

PICKERING: Yes. It's a fearful strain. I rather fancied myself because I can pronounce twenty-four distinct vowel sounds; but your hundred and thirty beat me. I cant hear a bit of difference between most of them.

HIGGINS (*chuckling, and going over to the piano to eat sweets*): Oh, that comes with practice. You hear no difference at first; but you keep on listening, and presently you find theyre all as different as A from B. (*Mrs Pearce looks in: she is Higgins's housekeeper.*) Whats the matter?

MRS PEARCE (*hesitating, evidently perplexed*): A young woman asks to see you, sir.

HIGGINS: A young woman! What does she want?

MRS PEARCE: Well, sir, she says youll be glad to see her when you know what she's come about. She's quite a common girl, sir. Very common indeed. I should have sent her away, only I thought perhaps you wanted her to talk into your machines. I hope Ive not done wrong; but really you see such queer people sometimes—youll excuse me, I'm sure, sir—

HIGGINS: Oh, thats all right, Mrs Pearce. Has she an interesting accent?

MRS PEARCE: Oh, something dreadful, sir, really. I dont know how you can take an interest in it.

HIGGINS (*to Pickering*): Lets have her up. Shew her up, Mrs Pearce (*he rushes across to his working table and picks out a cylinder to use on the phonograph*).

MRS PEARCE (*only half resigned to it*): Very well, sir. It's for you to say. (*She goes downstairs.*)

HIGGINS: This is rather a bit of luck. I'll shew you how I make records. We'll set her talking; and I'll take it down first in Bell's Visible Speech; then in broad Romic; and then we'll get her on the phonograph so that you can turn her on as often as you like with the written transcript before you.

MRS PEARCE (*returning*): This is the young woman.

(*The flower girl enters in state. She has a hat with three ostrich feathers, orange, sky-blue, and red. She has a nearly clean apron, and the shoddy coat has been tidied a little. The pathos of this deplorable figure, with its innocent vanity and consequential air, touches Pickering, who has already straightened himself in the presence of Mrs Pearce. But as to Higgins, the only distinction he makes between men and women is that when he is neither bul-*)

lying nor exclaiming to the heavens against some feather-weight cross, he coaxes women as a child coaxes its nurse when it wants to get anything out of her.)

HIGGINS (*brusquely, recognizing her with unconcealed disappointment, and at once, babylike, making an intolerable grievance of it*): Why, this is the girl I jotted down last night. She's no use: Ive got all the records I want of the Lisson Grove lingo; and I'm not going to waste another cylinder on it. (*To the girl*) Be off with you: I dont want you.

THE FLOWER GIRL: Dont you be so saucy. You aint heard what I come for yet. (*To Mrs Pearce, who is waiting at the door for further instructions*): Did you tell him I come in a taxi?

MRS PEARCE: Nonsense, girl! what do you think a gentleman like Mr Higgins cares what you came in?

THE FLOWER GIRL: Oh, we are proud! He aint above giving lessons, not him: I heard him say so. Well, I aint come here to ask for any compliment; and if my money's not good enough I can go elsewhere.

HIGGINS: Good enough for what?

THE FLOWER GIRL: Good enough for yǝ-oo. Now you know, dont you? I'm come to have lessons, I am. And to pay for em tǝ-oo: make no mistake.

HIGGINS (*stupent*): Well!!! (*Recovering his breath with a gasp*) What do you expect me to say to you?

THE FLOWER GIRL: Well, if you was a gentleman, you might ask me to sit down, I think. Dont I tell you I'm bringing you business?

HIGGINS: Pickering: shall we ask this baggage to sit down, or shall we throw her out of the window?

THE FLOWER GIRL (*running away in terror to the piano, where she turns at bay*): Ah-ah-oh-ow-ow-ow-oo! (*Wounded and whimpering*) I wont be called a baggage when Ive offered to pay like any lady.

(*Motionless, the two men stare at her from the other side of the room, amazed.*)

PICKERING (*gently*): But what is it you want?

THE FLOWER GIRL: I want to be a lady in a flower shop

stead of sellin at the corner of Tottenham Court Road.
But they wont take me unless I can talk more genteel.
He said he could teach me. Well, here I am ready to
pay him—not asking any favor—and he treats me zif I
was dirt.

MRS PEARCE: How can you be such a foolish ignorant
girl as to think you could afford to pay Mr Higgins?

THE FLOWER GIRL: Why shouldnt I? I know what lessons cost as well as you do; and I'm ready to pay.

HIGGINS: How much?

THE FLOWER GIRL (*coming back to him, triumphant*):
Now youre talking! I thought youd come off it when you
saw a chance of getting back a bit of what you chucked
at me last night. (*Confidentially*) Youd had a drop in,
hadnt you?

HIGGINS (*peremptorily*): Sit down.

THE FLOWER GIRL: Oh, if youre going to make a compliment of it—

HIGGINS (*thundering at her*): Sit down.

MRS PEARCE (*severely*): Sit down, girl. Do as youre
told.

THE FLOWER GIRL: Ah-ah-ah-ow-ow-oo! (*She stands,
half rebellious, half bewildered.*)

PICKERING (*very courteous*): Wont you sit down? (*He
places the stray chair near the hearthrug between himself
and Higgins.*)

LIZA (*coyly*): Dont mind if I do. (*She sits down. Pickering returns to the hearthrug.*)

HIGGINS: Whats your name?

THE FLOWER GIRL: Liza Doolittle.

HIGGINS (*declaiming gravely*):

Eliza, Elizabeth, Betsy and Bess,
They went to the woods to get a bird's nes':

PICKERING: They found a nest with four eggs in it:
HIGGINS: They took one apiece, and left three in it.
(*They laugh heartily at their own fun.*)
LIZA: Oh, dont be silly.

MRS PEARCE (*placing herself behind Eliza's chair*): You mustnt speak to the gentleman like that.

LIZA: Well, why wont he speak sensible to me?

HIGGINS: Come back to business. How much do you propose to pay me for the lessons?

LIZA: Oh, I know whats right. A lady friend of mine gets French lessons for eighteenpence an hour from a real French gentleman. Well, you wouldnt have the face to ask me the same for teaching me my own language as you would for French; so I wont give more than a shilling. Take it or leave it.

HIGGINS (*walking up and down the room, rattling his keys and his cash in his pockets*): You know, Pickering, if you consider a shilling, not as a simple shilling, but as a percentage of this girl's income, it works out as fully equivalent to sixty or seventy guineas from a millionaire.

PICKERING: How so?

HIGGINS: Figure it out. A millionaire has about £150 a day. She earns about half-a-crown.

LIZA (*haughtily*): Who told you I only—

HIGGINS (*continuing*): She offers me two-fifths of her day's income for a lesson. Two-fifths of a millionaire's income for a day would be somewhere about £60. It's handsome. By George, it's enormous! it's the biggest offer I ever had.

LIZA (*rising, terrified*): Sixty pounds! What are you talking about? I never offered you sixty pounds. Where would I get—

HIGGINS: Hold your tongue.

LIZA (*weeping*): But I aint got sixty pounds. Oh—

MRS PEARCE: Don't cry, you silly girl. Sit down. Nobody is going to touch your money.

HIGGINS: Somebody is going to touch you, with a broomstick, if you dont stop snivelling. Sit down.

LIZA: (*obeying slowly*): Ah-ah-ah-ow-oo-o! One would think you was my father.

HIGGINS: If I decide to teach you, I'll be worse than two fathers to you. Here (*he offers her his silk handkerchief!*).

LIZA: Whats this for?

HIGGINS: To wipe your eyes. To wipe any part of your face that feels moist. Remember: thats your handkerchief; and thats your sleeve. Dont mistake the one for the other if you wish to become a lady in a shop.

(*Liza, utterly bewildered, stares helplessly at him.*)

MRS PEARCE: It's no use talking to her like that, Mr Higgins: she doesnt understand you. Besides, youre quite wrong: she doesnt do it that way at all (*she takes the handkerchief*).

LIZA: (*snatching it*): Here! You give me that handkerchief. He gev it to me, not to you.

PICKERING (*laughing*): He did. I think it must be regarded as her property, Mrs Pearce.

MRS PEARCE (*resigning herself*): Serve you right, Mr Higgins.

PICKERING: Higgins: I'm interested. What about the ambassador's garden party? I'll say youre the greatest teacher alive if you make that good. I'll bet you all the expenses of the experiment you cant do it. And I'll pay for the lessons.

LIZA: Oh, you are real good. Thank you, Captain.

HIGGINS (*tempted, looking at her*): It's almost irresistible. She's so deliciously low—so horribly dirty—

LIZA (*protesting extremely*): Ah-ah-ah-ah-ow-ow-oo-oo!!! I aint dirty: I washed my face and hands afore I come, I did.

PICKERING: Youre certainly not going to turn her head with flattery, Higgins.

MRS PEARCE (*uneasy*): Oh, dont say that, sir: theres more ways than one of turning a girl's head; and nobody can do it better than Mr Higgins, though he may not always mean it. I do hope, sir, you wont encourage him to do anything foolish.

HIGGINS (*becoming excited as the idea grows on him*): What is life but a series of inspired follies? The difficulty is to find them to do. Never lose a chance: it doesnt come every day. I shall make a duchess of this draggletailed guttersnipe.

LIZA (*strongly deprecating this view of her*): Ah-ah-ah-ow-ow-oo!

HIGGINS (*carried away*): Yes: in six months—in three if she has a good ear and a quick tongue—I'll take her anywhere and pass her off as anything. We'll start today: now! this moment! Take her away and clean her, Mrs Pearce. Monkey Brand, if it wont come off any other way. Is there a good fire in the kitchen?

MRS PEARCE (*protesting*): Yes; but—

HIGGINS (*storming on*): Take all her clothes off and burn them. Ring up Whiteley or somebody for new ones. Wrap her up in brown paper til they come.

LIZA: Youre no gentleman, youre not, to talk of such things. I'm a good girl, I am; and I know what the like of you are, I do.

HIGGINS: We want none of your Lisson Grove prudery here, young woman. Youve got to learn to behave like a duchess. Take her away, Mrs Pearce. If she gives you any trouble, wallop her.

LIZA (*springing up and running between Pickering and Mrs Pearce for protection*): No! I'll call the police, I will.

MRS PEARCE: But Ive no place to put her.

HIGGINS: Put her in the dustbin.

LIZA: Ah-ah-ah-ow-ow-oo!

PICKERING: Oh come, Higgins! be reasonable.

MRS PEARCE (*resolutely*): You must be reasonable, Mr Higgins: really you must. You cant walk over everybody like this.

(*Higgins, thus scolded, subsides. The hurricane is succeeded by a zephyr of amiable surprise.*)

HIGGINS (*with professional exquisiteness of modulation*): *I* walk over everybody! My dear Mrs Pearce, my dear Pickering, I never had the slightest intention of walking over anyone. All I propose is that we should be kind to this poor girl. We must help her to prepare and fit herself for her new station in life. If I did not express myself clearly it was because I did not wish to hurt her delicacy, or yours.

(*Liza, reassured, steals back to her chair.*)

MRS PEARCE (*to Pickering*): Well, did you ever hear anything like that, sir?

PICKERING (*laughing heartily*): Never, Mrs Pearce: never.

HIGGINS (*patiently*): Whats the matter?

MRS PEARCE: Well, the matter is, sir, that you can't take a girl up like that as if you were picking up a pebble on the beach.

HIGGINS: Why not?

MRS PEARCE: Why not! But you dont know anything about her. What about her parents? She may be married.

LIZA: Garn!

HIGGINS: There! As the girl very properly says, Garn! Married indeed! Dont you know that a woman of that class looks a worn out drudge of fifty a year after she's married?

LIZA: Whood marry me?

HIGGINS (*suddenly resorting to the most thrillingly beautiful low tones in his best elocutionary style*): By George, Eliza, the streets will be strewn with the bodies of men shooting themselves for your sake before Ive done with you.

MRS PEARCE: Nonsense, sir. You mustnt talk like that to her.

LIZA (*rising and squaring herself determinedly*): I'm going away. He's off his chump, he is. I dont want no balmies teaching me.

HIGGINS (*wounded in his tenderest point by her insensibility to his elocution*): Oh, indeed! I'm mad, am I? Very well, Mrs Pearce: you neednt order the new clothes for her. Throw her out.

LIZA (*whimpering*): Nah-ow. You got no right to touch me.

MRS PEARCE: You see now what comes of being saucy. (*Indicating the door*) This way, please.

LIZA (*almost in tears*): I didnt want no clothes. I wouldnt have taken them (*she throws away the handkerchief*). I can buy my own clothes.

HIGGINS (*deftly retrieving the handkerchief and inter-*

cepting her on her reluctant way to the door): Youre an ungrateful wicked girl. This is my return for offering to take you out of the gutter and dress you beautifully and make a lady of you.

MRS PEARCE: Stop, Mr Higgins. I wont allow it. It's you that are wicked. Go home to your parents, girl; and tell them to take better care of you.

LIZA: I aint got no parents. They told me I was big enough to earn my own living and turned me out.

MRS PEARCE: Wheres your mother?

LIZA: I aint got no mother. Her that turned me out was my sixth stepmother. But I done without them. And I'm a good girl, I am.

HIGGINS: Very well, then, what on earth is all this fuss about? The girl doesnt belong to anybody—is no use of anybody but me. (*He goes to Mrs Pearce and begins coaxing.*) You can adopt her, Mrs Pearce: I'm sure a daughter would be a great amusement to you. Now dont make any more fuss. Take her downstairs; and—

MRS PEARCE: But whats to become of her? Is she to be paid anything? Do be sensible, sir.

HIGGINS: Oh, pay her whatever is necessary: put it down in the housekeeping book. (*Impatiently*) What on earth will she want with money? She'll have her food and her clothes. She'll only drink if you give her money.

LIZA (*turning on him*): Oh you are a brute. It's a lie: nobody ever saw the sign of liquor on me. (*To Pickering*) Oh, sir: youre a gentleman: dont let him speak to me like that.

PICKERING (*in good-humored remonstrance*): Does it occur to you, Higgins, that the girl has some feelings?

HIGGINS (*looking critically at her*): Oh no, I dont think so. Not any feelings that we need bother about. (*Cheerily*) Have you, Eliza?

LIZA: I got my feelings same as anyone else.

HIGGINS (*to Pickering, reflectively*): You see the difficulty?

PICKERING: Eh? What difficulty?

HIGGINS: To get her to talk grammar. The mere pronunciation is easy enough.

LIZA: I dont want to talk grammar. I want to talk like a lady in a flower shop.

MRS PEARCE: Will you please keep to the point, Mr Higgins. I want to know on what terms the girl is to be here. Is she to have any wages? And what is to become of her when youve finished your teaching? You must look ahead a little.

HIGGINS (*impatiently*): Whats to become of her if I leave her in the gutter? Tell me that, Mrs Pearce.

MRS PEARCE: Thats her own business, not yours, Mr Higgins.

HIGGINS: Well, when Ive done with her, we can throw her back into the gutter; and then it will be her own business again; so thats all right.

LIZA: Oh, youve no feeling heart in you; you dont care for nothing but yourself. (*She rises and takes the floor resolutely.*) Here! Ive had enough of this. I'm going (*making for the door*). You ought to be ashamed of yourself, you ought.

HIGGINS (*snatching a chocolate cream from the piano, his eyes suddenly beginning to twinkle with mischief*): Have some chocolates, Eliza.

LIZA (*halting, tempted*): How do I know what might be in them? Ive heard of girls being drugged by the likes of you.

(*Higgins whips out his penknife; cuts a chocolate in two; puts one half into his mouth and bolts it; and offers her the other half.*)

HIGGINS: Pledge of good faith, Eliza. I eat one half: you eat the other. (*Liza opens her mouth to retort: he pops the half chocolate into it.*) You shall have boxes of them, barrels of them, every day. You shall live on them. Eh?

LIZA (*who has disposed of the chocolate after being nearly choked by it*): I wouldnt have ate it, only I'm too ladylike to take it out of my mouth.

HIGGINS: Listen, Eliza. I think you said you came in a taxi.

LIZA: Well, what if I did? Ive as good a right to take a taxi as anyone else.

HIGGINS: You have, Eliza; and in future you shall have as many taxis as you want. You shall go up and down and round the town in a taxi every day. Think of that, Eliza.

MRS PEARCE: Mr Higgins: youre tempting the girl. It's not right. She should think of the future.

HIGGINS: At her age! Nonsense! Time enough to think of the future when you havent any future to think of. No, Eliza: do as this lady does: think of other people's futures; but never think of your own. Think of chocolates, and taxis, and gold, and diamonds.

LIZA: No: I dont want no gold and no diamonds. I'm a good girl, I am. (*She sits down again, with an attempt at dignity.*)

HIGGINS: You shall remain so, Eliza, under the care of Mrs Pearce. And you shall marry an officer in the Guards, with a beautiful moustache: the son of a marquis, who will disinherit him for marrying you, but will relent when he sees your beauty and goodness—

PICKERING: Excuse me, Higgins; but I really must interfere. Mrs Pearce is quite right. If this girl is to put herself in your hands for six months for an experiment in teaching, she must understand thoroughly what she's doing.

HIGGINS: How can she? She's incapable of understanding anything. Besides, do any of us understand what we are doing? If we did, would we ever do it?

PICKERING: Very clever, Higgins; but not to the present point. (*To Eliza*) Miss Doolittle—

LIZA (*overwhelmed*): Ah-ah-ow-oo!

HIGGINS: There! Thats all youll get out of Eliza. Ah-ah-ow-oo! No use explaining. As a military man you ought to know that. Give her her orders: thats enough for her. Eliza: you are to live here for the next six months, learning how to speak beautifully, like a lady in

a florist's shop. If youre good and do whatever youre
told, you shall sleep in a proper bedroom, and have lots
to eat, and money to buy chocolates and take rides in
taxis. If youre naughty and idle you will sleep in the
back kitchen among the black beetles, and be walloped
by Mrs Pearce with a broomstick. At the end of six
months you shall go to Buckingham Palace in a carriage,
beautifully dressed. If the King finds out youre not a
lady, you will be taken by the police to the Tower of
London, where your head will be cut off as a warning
to other presumptuous flower girls. If you are not found
out, you shall have a present of seven-and-sixpence to
start life with as a lady in a shop. If you refuse this offer
you will be a most ungrateful wicked girl; and the angels
will weep for you. (*To Pickering*) Now are you satisfied,
Pickering? (*To Mrs Pearce*) Can I put it more plainly
and fairly, Mrs Pearce?

MRS PEARCE (*patiently*): I think youd better let me
speak to the girl properly in private. I dont know that I
can take charge of her or consent to the arrangement at
all. Of course I know you dont mean her any harm; but
when you get what you call interested in people's accents, you never think or care what may happen to them
or you. Come with me, Eliza.

HIGGINS: Thats all right. Thank you, Mrs Pearce. Bundle her off to the bathroom.

LIZA (*rising reluctantly and suspiciously*): Youre a
great bully, you are. I wont stay here if I dont like. I
wont let nobody wallop me. I never asked to go to Bucknam Palace, I didnt. I was never in trouble with the
police, not me. I'm a good girl—

MRS PEARCE: Dont answer back, girl. You dont understand the gentleman. Come with me. (*She leads the way
to the door, and holds it open for Eliza.*)

LIZA (*as she goes out*): Well, what I say is right. I wont
go near the King, not if I'm going to have my head cut
off. If I'd known what I was letting myself in for, I
wouldnt have come here. I always been a good girl; and
I never offered to say a word to him; and I dont owe

him nothing; and I dont care; and I wont be put upon; and I have my feelings the same as anyone else—

(*Mrs Pearce shuts the door; and Eliza's plaints are no longer audible.*)

* * *

Eliza is taken upstairs to the third floor greatly to her surprise; for she expected to be taken down to the scullery. There Mrs Pearce opens a door and takes her into a spare bedroom.

MRS PEARCE: I will have to put you here. This will be your bedroom.

LIZA: O-h, I couldnt sleep here, missus. It's too good for the likes of me. I should be afraid to touch anything. I aint a duchess yet, you know.

MRS PEARCE: You have got to make yourself as clean as the room: then you wont be afraid of it. And you must call me Mrs Pearce, not missus. (*She throws open the door of the dressingroom, now modernized as a bathroom.*)

LIZA: Gawd! whats this? Is this where you wash clothes? Funny sort of copper I call it.

MRS PEARCE: It is not a copper. This is where we wash ourselves, Eliza, and where I am going to wash you.

LIZA: You expect me to get into that and wet myself all over! Not me. I should catch my death. I knew a woman did it every Saturday night; and she died of it.

MRS PEARCE: Mr Higgins has the gentlemen's bathroom downstairs; and he has a bath every morning, in cold water.

LIZA: Ugh! He's made of iron, that man.

MRS PEARCE: If you are to sit with him and the Colonel and be taught you will have to do the same. They wont like the smell of you if you dont. But you can have the water as hot as you like. There are two taps: hot and cold.

LIZA (*weeping*): I couldnt. I dursnt. It's not natural: it would kill me. Ive never had a bath in my life: not what youd call a proper one.

MRS PEARCE: Well, dont you want to be clean and sweet and decent, like a lady? You know you cant be a nice girl inside if youre a dirty slut outside.

LIZA: Boohoo!!!!

MRS PEARCE: Now stop crying and go back into your room and take off all your clothes. Then wrap yourself in this (*taking down a gown from its peg and handing it to her*) and come back to me. I will get the bath ready.

LIZA (*all tears*): I cant. I wont. I'm not used to it. Ive never took off all my clothes before. It's not right: it's not decent.

MRS PEARCE: Nonsense, child. Dont you take off all your clothes every night when you go to bed?

LIZA (*amazed*): No. Why should I? I should catch my death. Of course I take off my skirt.

MRS PEARCE: Do you mean that you sleep in the underclothes you wear in the daytime?

LIZA: What else have I to sleep in?

MRS PEARCE: You will never do that again as long as you live here. I will get you a proper nightdress.

LIZA: Do you mean change into cold things and lie awake shivering half the night? You want to kill me, you do.

MRS PEARCE: I want to change you from a frowzy slut to a clean respectable girl fit to sit with the gentlemen in the study. Are you going to trust me and do what I tell you or be thrown out and sent back to your flower basket?

LIZA: But you dont know what the cold is to me. You dont know how I dread it.

MRS PEARCE: Your bed wont be cold here: I will put a hot water bottle in it. (*Pushing her into the bedroom*) Off with you and undress.

LIZA: Oh, if only I'd a known what a dreadful thing it is to be clean I'd never have come. I didnt know when I was well off. I—(*Mrs Pearce pushes her through the door, but leaves it partly open lest her prisoner should take to flight.*

(*Mrs Pearce puts on a pair of white rubber sleeves, and*

fills the bath, mixing hot and cold, and testing the result with the bath thermometer. She perfumes it with a handful of bath salts and adds a palmful of mustard. She then takes a formidable looking long handled scrubbing brush and soaps it profusely with a ball of scented soap.

(*Eliza comes back with nothing on but the bath gown huddled tightly round her, a piteous spectacle of abject terror.*)

MRS PEARCE: Now come along. Take that thing off.

LIZA: Oh I couldnt, Mrs Pearce: I reely couldnt. I never done such a thing.

MRS PEARCE: Nonsense. Here: step in and tell me whether it's hot enough for you.

LIZA: Ah-oo! Ah-oo! It's too hot.

MRS PEARCE (*deftly snatching the gown away and throwing Eliza down on her back*): It wont hurt you. (*She sets to work with the scrubbing brush.*)

(*Eliza's screams are heartrending.*)

* * *

Meanwhile the Colonel has been having it out with Higgins about Eliza. Pickering has come from the hearth to the chair and seated himself astride of it with his arms on the back to cross-examine him.

PICKERING: Excuse the straight question, Higgins. Are you a man of good character where women are concerned?

HIGGINS (*moodily*): Have you ever met a man of good character where women are concerned?

PICKERING: Yes: very frequently.

HIGGINS (*dogmatically, lifting himself on his hands to the level of the piano, and sitting on it with a bounce*): Well, I havnt. I find that the moment I let a woman make friends with me, she becomes jealous, exacting, suspicious, and a damned nuisance. I find that the moment I let myself make friends with a woman, I become selfish and tyrannical. Women upset everything. When you let them into your life, you find that the woman is driving at one thing and youre driving at another.

PICKERING: At what, for example?

HIGGINS (*coming off the piano restlessly*): Oh, Lord knows! I suppose the woman wants to live her own life; and the man wants to live his; and each tries to drag the other on to the wrong track. One wants to go north and the other south; and the result is that both have to go east, though they both hate the east wind. (*He sits down on the bench at the keyboard.*) So here I am, a confirmed old bachelor, and likely to remain so.

PICKERING (*rising and standing over him gravely*): Come, Higgins! You know what I mean. If I'm to be in this business I shall feel responsible for that girl. I hope it's understood that no advantage is to be taken of her position.

HIGGINS: What! That thing! Sacred, I assure you. (*Rising to explain*) You see, she'll be a pupil; and teaching would be impossible unless pupils were sacred. Ive taught scores of American millionairesses how to speak English: the best-looking women in the world. I'm seasoned. They might as well be blocks of wood. *I* might as well be a block of wood. It's—

(*Mrs Pearce opens the door. She has Eliza's hat in her hand. Pickering retires to the easy-chair at the hearth and sits down.*)

HIGGINS (*eagerly*): Well, Mrs Pearce: is it all right?

MRS PEARCE (*at the door*): I just wish to trouble you with a word, if I may, Mr Higgins.

HIGGINS: Yes, certainly. Come in. (*She comes forward.*) Dont burn that, Mrs Pearce. I'll keep it as a curiosity. (*He takes the hat.*)

MRS PEARCE: Handle it carefully, sir, please. I had to promise her not to burn it; but I had better put it in the oven for a while.

HIGGINS (*putting it down hastily on the piano*): Oh! thank you. Well, what have you to say to me?

PICKERING: Am I in the way?

MRS PEARCE: Not at all, sir. Mr Higgins: will you please be very particular what you say before the girl?

HIGGINS (*sternly*): Of course. I'm always particular about what I say. Why do you say this to me?

MRS PEARCE (*unmoved*): No, sir: youre not at all particular when youve mislaid anything or when you get a little impatient. Now it doesnt matter before me: I'm used to it. But you really must not swear before the girl.

HIGGINS (*indignantly*): I swear! (*Most emphatically*) I never swear. I detest the habit. What the devil do you mean?

MRS PEARCE (*stolidly*): Thats what I mean, sir. You swear a great deal too much. I dont mind your damning and blasting, and what the devil and where the devil and who the devil—

HIGGINS: Mrs Pearce: this language from your lips! Really!

MRS PEARCE (*not to be put off*):—but there is a certain word I must ask you not to use. The girl used it herself when she began to enjoy the bath. It begins with the same letter as bath. She knows no better: she learnt it at her mother's knee. But she must not hear it from your lips.

HIGGINS (*loftily*): I cannot charge myself with having ever uttered it, Mrs Pearce. (*She looks at him steadfastly. He adds, hiding an uneasy conscience with a judicial air*) Except perhaps in a moment of extreme and justifiable excitement.

MRS PEARCE: Only this morning, sir, you applied it to your boots, to the butter, and to the brown bread.

HIGGINS: Oh, that! Mere alliteration, Mrs Pearce, natural to a poet.

MRS PEARCE: Well, sir, whatever you choose to call it, I beg you not to let the girl hear you repeat it.

HIGGINS: Oh, very well, very well. Is that all?

MRS PEARCE: No, sir. We shall have to be very particular with this girl as to personal cleanliness.

HIGGINS: Certainly. Quite right. Most important.

MRS PEARCE: I mean not to be slovenly about her dress or untidy in leaving things about.

HIGGINS (*going to her solemnly*): Just so. I intended to

call your attention to that. (*He passes on to Pickering, who is enjoying the conversation immensely.*) It is these little things that matter, Pickering. Take care of the pence and the pounds will take care of themselves is as true of personal habits as of money. (*He comes to anchor on the hearthrug, with the air of a man in an unassailable position.*)

MRS PEARCE: Yes, sir. Then might I ask you not to come down to breakfast in your dressing-gown, or at any rate not to use it as a napkin to the extent you do, sir. And if you would be so good as not to eat everything off the same plate, and to remember not to put the porridge saucepan out of your hand on the clean tablecloth, it would be a better example to the girl. You know you nearly choked yourself with a fishbone in the jam only last week.

HIGGINS (*routed from the hearthrug and drifting back to the piano*): I may do these things sometimes in absence of mind; but surely I dont do them habitually. (*Angrily*) By the way: my dressing-gown smells most damnably of benzine.

MRS PEARCE: No doubt it does, Mr Higgins. But if you will wipe your fingers—

HIGGINS (*yelling*): Oh very well, very well: I'll wipe them in my hair in future.

MRS PEARCE: I hope youre not offended, Mr Higgins.

HIGGINS (*shocked at finding himself thought capable of an unamiable sentiment*): Not at all, not at all. Youre quite right, Mrs Pearce: I shall be particularly careful before the girl. Is that all?

MRS PEARCE: No, sir. Might she use some of those Japanese dresses you brought from abroad? I really cant put her back into her old things.

HIGGINS: Certainly. Anything you like. Is that all?

MRS PEARCE: Thank you, sir. Thats all. (*She goes out.*)

HIGGINS: You know, Pickering, that woman has the most extraordinary ideas about me. Here I am, a shy, diffident sort of man. Ive never been able to feel really grown-up and tremendous, like other chaps. And yet she's firmly persuaded that I'm an arbitrary overbearing bossing kind of person. I cant account for it.

(*Mrs Pearce returns.*)

MRS PEARCE: If you please, sir, the trouble's beginning already. Theres a dustman downstairs, Alfred Doolittle, wants to see you. He says you have his daughter here.

PICKERING (*rising*): Phew! I say!

HIGGINS (*promptly*): Send the blackguard up.

MRS PEARCE: Oh, very well, sir. (*She goes out.*)

PICKERING: He may not be a blackguard, Higgins.

HIGGINS: Nonsense. Of course he's a blackguard.

PICKERING: Whether he is or not, I'm afraid we shall have some trouble with him.

HIGGINS (*confidently*): Oh no: I think not. If theres any trouble he shall have it with me, not I with him. And we are sure to get something interesting out of him.

PICKERING: About the girl?

HIGGINS: No. I mean his dialect.

PICKERING: Oh!

MRS PEARCE (*at the door*): Doolittle, sir. (*She admits Doolittle and retires.*)

(*Alfred Doolittle is an elderly but vigorous dustman, clad in the costume of his profession, including a hat with a back brim covering his neck and shoulders. He has well marked and rather interesting features, and seems equally free from fear and conscience. He has a remarkably expressive voice, the result of a habit of giving vent to his feelings without reserve. His present pose is that of wounded honor and stern resolution.*)

DOOLITTLE (*at the door, uncertain which of the two gentlemen is his man*): Professor Iggins?

HIGGINS: Here. Good morning. Sit down.

DOOLITTLE: Morning, Governor. (*He sits down magisterially.*) I come about a very serious matter, Governor.

HIGGINS (*to Pickering*): Brought up in Hounslow. Mother Welsh, I should think. (*Doolittle opens his mouth, amazed. Higgins continues*) What do you want, Doolittle?

DOOLITTLE (*menacingly*): I want my daughter: thats what I want. See?

HIGGINS: Of course you do. Youre her father, arnt you? You dont suppose anyone else wants her, do you? I'm glad to see you have some spark of family feeling left. She's upstairs. Take her away at once.

DOOLITTLE (*rising, fearfully taken aback*): What!

HIGGINS: Take her away. Do you suppose I'm going to keep your daughter for you?

DOOLITTLE (*remonstrating*): Now, now, look here, Governor. Is this reasonable? Is it fairity to take advantage of a man like this? The girl belongs to me. You got her. Where do I come in? (*He sits down again.*)

HIGGINS: Your daughter had the audacity to come to my house and ask me to teach her how to speak properly so that she could get a place in a flower shop. This gentleman and my housekeeper have been here all the time. (*Bullying him*) How dare you come here and attempt to blackmail me? You sent her here on purpose.

DOOLITTLE (*protesting*): No, Governor.

HIGGINS: You must have. How else could you possibly know that she is here?

DOOLITTLE: Dont take a man up like that, Governor.

HIGGINS: The police shall take you up. This is a plant— a plot to extort money by threats. I shall telephone for the police (*he goes resolutely to the telephone and opens the directory*).

DOOLITTLE: Have I asked you for a brass farthing? I leave it to the gentleman here: have I said a word about money?

HIGGINS (*throwing the book aside and marching down on Doolittle with a poser*): What else did you come for?

DOOLITTLE (*sweetly*): Well, what would a man come for? Be human, Governor.

HIGGINS (*disarmed*): Alfred: did you put her up to it?

DOOLITTLE: So help me, Governor, I never did. I take my Bible oath I aint seen the girl these two months past.

HIGGINS: Then how did you know she was here?

DOOLITTLE (*"most musical, most melancholy"*): I'll tell

you, Governor, if youll only let me get a word in. I'm willing to tell you. I'm wanting to tell you. I'm waiting to tell you.

HIGGINS: Pickering: this chap has a certain natural gift of rhetoric. Observe the rhythm of his native woodnotes wild. "I'm willing to tell you: I'm wanting to tell you: I'm waiting to tell you." Sentimental rhetoric! thats the Welsh strain in him. It also accounts for his mendacity and dishonesty.

PICKERING: Oh, please, Higgins: I'm west country myself. (*To Doolittle*) How did you know the girl was here if you didnt send her?

DOOLITTLE: It was like this, Governor. The girl took a boy in the taxi to give him a jaunt. Son of her landlady, he is. He hung about on the chance of her giving him another ride home. Well, she sent him back for her luggage when she heard you was willing for her to stop here. I met the boy at the corner of Long Acre and Endell Street.

HIGGINS: Public house. Yes?

DOOLITTLE: The poor man's club, Governor: why shouldnt I?

PICKERING: Do let him tell his story, Higgins.

DOOLITTLE: He told me what was up. And I ask you, what was my feelings and my duty as a father? I says to the boy, "You bring me the luggage," I says—

PICKERING: Why didnt you go for it yourself?

DOOLITTLE: Landlady wouldnt have trusted me with it, Governor. She's that kind of woman: you know. I had to give the boy a penny afore he trusted me with it, the little swine. I brought it to her just to oblige you like, and make myself agreeable. Thats all.

HIGGINS: How much luggage?

DOOLITTLE: Musical instrument, Governor. A few pictures, a trifle of jewelry, and a bird-cage. She said she didnt want no clothes. What was I to think from that, Governor? I ask you as a parent what was I to think?

HIGGINS: So you came to rescue her from worse than death, eh?

DOOLITTLE (*appreciatively: relieved at being so well understood*): Just so, Governor. Thats right.

PICKERING: But why did you bring her luggage if you intended to take her away?

DOOLITTLE: Have I said a word about taking her away? Have I now?

HIGGINS (*determinedly*): Youre going to take her away, double quick. (*He crosses to the hearth and rings the bell.*)

DOOLITTLE (*rising*): No, Governor. Dont say that. I'm not the man to stand in my girl's light. Heres a career opening for her, as you might say; and—

(*Mrs Pearce opens the door and awaits orders.*)

HIGGINS: Mrs Pearce: this is Eliza's father. He has come to take her away. Give her to him. (*He goes back to the piano, with an air of washing his hands of the whole affair.*)

DOOLITTLE: No. This is a misunderstanding. Listen here—

MRS PEARCE: He cant take her away, Mr Higgins: how can he? You told me to burn her clothes.

DOOLITTLE: Thats right. I cant carry the girl through the streets like a blooming monkey, can I? I put it to you.

HIGGINS: You have put it to me that you want your daughter. Take your daughter. If she has no clothes go out and buy her some.

DOOLITTLE (*desperate*): Wheres the clothes she come in? Did I burn them or did your missus here?

MRS PEARCE: I am the housekeeper, if you please. I have sent for some clothes for your girl. When they come you can take her away. You can wait in the kitchen. This way, please.

(*Doolittle, much troubled, accompanies her to the door; then hesitates; finally turns confidentially to Higgins.*)

DOOLITTLE: Listen here, Governor. You and me is men of the world aint we?

HIGGINS: Oh! Men of the world, are we? Youd better go, Mrs Pearce.

MRS PEARCE: I think so, indeed, sir. (*She goes, with dignity.*)

PICKERING: The floor is yours, Mr Doolittle.

DOOLITTLE (*to Pickering*): I thank you, Governor. (*To Higgins, who takes refuge on the piano bench, a little overwhelmed by the proximity of his visitor; for Doolittle has a professional flavor of dust about him.*) Well, the truth is, Ive taken a sort of fancy to you, Governor; and if you want the girl, I'm not so set on having her back home again but what I might be open to an arrangement. Regarded in the light of a young woman, she's a fine handsome girl. As a daughter she's not worth her keep; and so I tell you straight. All I ask is my rights as a father; and youre the last man alive to expect me to let her go for nothing; for I can see youre one of the straight sort, Governor. Well, whats a five-pound note to you? and whats Eliza to me? (*He turns to his chair and sits down judicially.*)

PICKERING: I think you ought to know, Doolittle, that Mr Higgins's intentions are entirely honorable.

DOOLITTLE: Course they are, Governor. If I thought they wasnt, I'd ask fifty.

HIGGINS (*revolted*): Do you mean to say that you would sell your daughter for £50?

DOOLITTLE: Not in a general way I wouldn't; but to oblige a gentleman like you I'd do a good deal, I do assure you.

PICKERING: Have you no morals, man?

DOOLITTLE (*unabashed*): Cant afford them, Governor. Neither could you if you was as poor as me. Not that I mean any harm, you know. But if Liza is going to have a bit out of this, why not me too?

HIGGINS (*troubled*): I dont know what to do, Pickering. There can be no question that as a matter of morals it's a positive crime to give this chap a farthing. And yet I feel a sort of rough justice in his claim.

DOOLITTLE: Thats it, Governor. Thats all I say. A father's heart, as it were.

PICKERING: Well, I know the feeling; but really it seems hardly right—

DOOLITTLE: Dont say that, Governor. Dont look at it that way. What am I, Governors both? I ask you, what am I? I'm one of the undeserving poor: thats what I am. Think of what that means to a man. It means that he's up agen middle class morality all the time. If theres anything going, and I put in for a bit of it, it's always the same story: "Youre undeserving; so you cant have it." But my needs is as great as the most deserving widow's that ever got money out of six different charities in one week for the death of the same husband. I dont need less than a deserving man: I need more. I dont eat less hearty than him; and I drink a lot more. I want a bit of amusement, cause I'm a thinking man. I want cheerfulness and a song and a band when I feel low. Well, they charge me just the same for everything as they charge the deserving. What is middle class morality? Just an excuse for never giving me anything. Therefore, I ask you, as two gentlemen, not to play that game on me. I'm playing straight with you. I aint pretending to be deserving. I'm undeserving; and I mean to go on being undeserving. I like it; and thats the truth. Will you take advantage of a man's nature to do him out of the price of his own daughter what he's brought up and fed and clothed by the sweat of his brow until she's growed big enough to be interesting to you two gentlemen? Is five pounds unreasonable? I put it to you; and I leave it to you.

HIGGINS (*rising, and going over to Pickering*): Pickering: if we were to take this man in hand for three months, he could choose between a seat in the Cabinet and a popular pulpit in Wales.

PICKERING: What do you say to that, Doolittle?

DOOLITTLE: Not me, Governor, thank you kindly. Ive heard all the preachers and all the prime ministers—for

I'm a thinking man and game for politics or religion or social reform same as all the other amusements—and I tell you it's a dog's life any way you look at it. Undeserving poverty is my line. Taking one station in society with another, it's—it's—well, it's the only one that has any ginger in it, to my taste.

HIGGINS: I suppose we must give him a fiver.

PICKERING: He'll make a bad use of it, I'm afraid.

DOOLITTLE: Not me, Governor, so help me I wont. Dont you be afraid that I'll save it and spare it and live idle on it. There wont be a penny of it left by Monday: I'll have to go to work same as if I'd never had it. It wont pauperize me, you bet. Just one good spree for myself and the missus, giving pleasure to ourselves and employment to others, and satisfaction to you to think it's not been throwed away. You couldnt spend it better.

HIGGINS (*taking out his pocket book and coming between Doolittle and the piano*): This is irresistible. Lets give him ten. (*He offers two notes to the dustman.*)

DOOLITTLE: No, Governor. She wouldnt have the heart to spend ten; and perhaps I shouldnt neither. Ten pounds is a lot of money: it makes a man feel prudent like; and then goodbye to happiness. You give me what I ask you, Governor: not a penny more, and not a penny less.

PICKERING: Why dont you marry that missus of yours? I rather draw the line at encouraging that sort of immorality.

DOOLITTLE: Tell her so, Governor: tell her so. I'm willing. It's me that suffers by it. Ive no hold on her. I got to be agreeable to her. I got to give her presents. I got to buy her clothes something sinful. I'm a slave to that woman, Governor, just because I'm not her lawful husband. And she knows it too. Catch her marrying me! Take my advice, Governor: marry Eliza while she's young and dont know no better. If you dont youll be sorry for it after. If you do, she'll be sorry for it after; but better her than you, because youre a man, and she's only a woman and dont know how to be happy anyhow.

HIGGINS: Pickering: if we listen to this man another minute, we shall have no convictions left. (*To Doolittle*) Five pounds I think you said.

DOOLITTLE: Thank you kindly, Governor.

HIGGINS: Youre sure you wont take ten?

DOOLITTLE: Not now. Another time, Governor.

HIGGINS (*handing him a five-pound note*): Here you are.

DOOLITTLE: Thank you, Governor. Good morning. (*He hurries to the door, anxious to get away with his booty. When he opens it he is confronted with a dainty and exquisitely clean young Japanese lady in a simple blue cotton kimono printed cunningly with small white jasmine blossoms. Mrs Pearce is with her. He gets out of her way deferentially and apologizes.*) Beg pardon, miss.

THE JAPANESE LADY: Garn! Dont you know your own daughter?

DOOLITTLE	*exclaiming*	Bly me! it's Eliza!
HIGGINS	*simul-*	Whats that? This!
PICKERING	*taneously*	By Jove!

LIZA: Dont I look silly?

HIGGINS: Silly?

MRS PEARCE (*at the door*): Now, Mr Higgins, please dont say anything to make the girl conceited about herself.

HIGGINS (*conscientiously*): Oh! Quite right, Mrs Pearce. (*To Eliza*) Yes: damned silly.

MRS PEARCE: Please, sir.

HIGGINS (*correcting himself*): I mean extremely silly.

LIZA: I should look all right with my hat on. (*She takes up her hat; puts it on; and walks across the room to the fireplace with a fashionable air.*)

HIGGINS: A new fashion, by George! And it ought to look horrible!

DOOLITTLE (*with fatherly pride*): Well, I never thought she'd clean up as good looking as that, Governor. She's a credit to me, aint she?

LIZA: I tell you, it's easy to clean up here. Hot and cold water on tap, just as much as you like, there is. Woolly towels, there is; and a towel horse so hot, it burns your fingers. Soft brushes to scrub yourself, and a wooden bowl of soap smelling like primroses. Now I know why ladies is so clean. Washing's a treat for them. Wish they could see what it is for the like of me!

HIGGINS: I'm glad the bathroom met with your approval.

LIZA: It didnt: not all of it; and I dont care who hears me say it. Mrs Pearce knows.

HIGGINS: What was wrong, Mrs Pearce?

MRS PEARCE (*blandly*): Oh, nothing, sir. It doesnt matter.

LIZA: I had a good mind to break it. I didnt know which way to look. But I hung a towel over it, I did.

HIGGINS: Over what?

MRS PEARCE: Over the looking-glass, sir.

HIGGINS: Doolittle: you have brought your daughter up too strictly.

DOOLITTLE: Me! I never brought her up at all, except to give her a lick of a strap now and again. Dont put it on me, Governor. She aint accustomed to it, you see: thats all. But she'll soon pick up your free-and-easy ways.

LIZA: I'm a good girl, I am; and I wont pick up no free-and-easy ways.

HIGGINS: Eliza: if you say again that youre a good girl, your father shall take you home.

LIZA: Not him. You dont know my father. All he come here for was to touch you for some money to get drunk on.

DOOLITTLE: Well, what else would I want money for? To put into the plate in church, I suppose. (*She puts out her tongue at him. He is so incensed by this that Pickering presently finds it necessary to step between them.*) Dont you give me none of your lip; and dont let me hear you giving this gentleman any of it neither, or youll hear from me about it. See?

HIGGINS: Have you any further advice to give her before you go, Doolittle? Your blessing, for instance.

DOOLITTLE: No, Governor: I aint such a mug as to put up my children to all I know myself. Hard enough to hold them in without that. If you want Eliza's mind improved, Governor, you do it yourself with a strap. So long, gentlemen. (*He turns to go.*)

HIGGINS (*impressively*): Stop. Youll come regularly to see your daughter. It's your duty, you know. My brother is a clergyman; and he could help you in your talks with her.

DOOLITTLE (*evasively*): Certainly, I'll come, Governor. Not just this week, because I have a job at a distance. But later on you may depend on me. Afternoon, gentlemen. Afternoon, maam. (*He touches his hat to Mrs Pearce, who disdains the salutation and goes out. He winks at Higgins, thinking him probably a fellow sufferer from Mrs Pearce's difficult disposition, and follows her.*)

LIZA: Dont you believe the old liar. He'd as soon you set a bulldog on him as a clergyman. You wont see him again in a hurry.

HIGGINS: I dont want to, Eliza. Do you?

LIZA: Not me. I dont want never to see him again, I dont. He's a disgrace to me, he is, collecting dust, instead of working at his trade.

PICKERING: What is his trade, Eliza?

LIZA: Talking money out of other people's pockets into his own. His proper trade's a navvy; and he works at it sometimes too—for exercise—and earns good money at it. Aint you going to call me Miss Doolittle any more?

PICKERING: I beg your pardon, Miss Doolittle. It was a slip of the tongue.

LIZA: Oh, I dont mind; only it sounded so genteel. I should just like to take a taxi to the corner of Tottenham Court Road and get out there and tell it to wait for me, just to put the girls in their place a bit. I wouldnt speak to them, you know.

PICKERING: Better wait til we get you something really fashionable.

HIGGINS: Besides, you shouldnt cut your old friends now that you have risen in the world. Thats what we call snobbery.

LIZA: You dont call the like of them my friends now, I should hope. Theyve took it out of me often enough with their ridicule when they had the chance; and now I mean to get a bit of my own back. But if I'm to have fashionable clothes, I'll wait. I should like to have some. Mrs Pearce says youre going to give me some to wear in bed at night different to what I wear in the daytime; but it do seem a waste of money when you could get something to shew. Besides, I never could fancy changing into cold things on a winter night.

MRS PEARCE (*coming back*): Now, Eliza. The new things have come for you to try on.

LIZA: Ah-ow-oo-ooh! (*She rushes out.*)

MRS PEARCE (*following her*): Oh, dont rush about like that, girl. (*She shuts the door behind her.*)

HIGGINS: Pickering: we have taken on a stiff job.

PICKERING (*with conviction*): Higgins: we have.

*   *   *

There seems to be some curiosity as to what Higgins's lessons to Eliza were like. Well, here is a sample: the first one.

Picture Eliza, in her new clothes, and feeling her inside put out of step by a lunch, dinner, and breakfast of a kind to which it is unaccustomed, seated with Higgins and the Colonel in the study, feeling like a hospital outpatient at a first encounter with the doctors.

Higgins, constitutionally unable to sit still, discomposes her still more by striding restlessly about. But for the reassuring presence and quietude of her friend the Colonel she would run for her life, even back to Drury Lane.

HIGGINS: Say your alphabet.

LIZA: I know my alphabet. Do you think I know nothing? I dont need to be taught like a child.

HIGGINS (*thundering*): Say your alphabet.

PICKERING: Say it, Miss Doolittle. You will understand presently. Do what he tells you; and let him teach you in his own way.

LIZA: Oh well, if you put it like that—Ahyee, bəyee, cəyee, dəyee—

HIGGINS (*with the roar of a wounded lion*): Stop. Listen to this, Pickering. This is what we pay for as elementary education. This unfortunate animal has been locked up for nine years in school at our expense to teach her to speak and read the language of Shakespear and Milton. And the result is Ahyee, Bə-yee, Cə-yee, Də-yee. (*To Eliza*) Say A, B, C, D.

LIZA (*almost in tears*): But I'm sayin it. Ahyee, Bəyee, Cəyee—

HIGGINS: Stop. Say a cup of tea.

LIZA: A cappətə-ee.

HIGGINS: Put your tongue forward until it squeezes against the top of your lower teeth. Now say cup.

LIZA: C-c-c—I cant. C-Cup.

PICKERING: Good. Splendid, Miss Doolittle.

HIGGINS: By Jupiter, she's done it at the first shot. Pickering: we shall make a duchess of her. (*To Eliza*) Now do you think you could possibly say tea? Not tə-yee, mind: if you ever say bə-yee cə-yee də-yee again you shall be dragged round the room three times by the hair of your head. (*Fortissimo*) T, T, T, T.

LIZA (*weeping*): I cant hear no difference cep that it sounds more genteel-like when you say it.

HIGGINS: Well, if you can hear that difference, what the devil are you crying for? Pickering: give her a chocolate.

PICKERING: No, no. Never mind crying a little, Miss Doolittle: you are doing very well; and the lessons wont hurt. I promise you I wont let him drag you round the room by your hair.

HIGGINS: Be off with you to Mrs Pearce and tell her about it. Think about it. Try to do it by yourself: and keep your tongue well forward in your mouth instead of trying to roll it up and swallow it. Another lesson at half-past four this afternoon. Away with you.

(*Eliza, still sobbing, rushes from the room.*)

And that is the sort of ordeal poor Eliza has to go through for months before we meet her again on her first appearance in London society of the professional class.

ACT THREE

It is Mrs Higgins's at-home day. Nobody has yet arrived.
Her drawing room, in a flat on Chelsea Embankment,
has three windows looking on the river; and the ceiling
is not so lofty as it would be in an older house of the
same pretension. The windows are open, giving access to
a balcony with flowers in pots. If you stand with your
face to the windows, you have the fireplace on your left
and the door in the right-hand wall close to the corner
nearest the windows.

Mrs Higgins was brought up on Morris and Burne
Jones; and her room, which is very unlike her son's room
in Wimpole Street, is not crowded with furniture and little
tables and nicknacks. In the middle of the room there is
a big ottoman; and this, with the carpet, the Morris wall-
papers, and the Morris chintz window curtains and bro-
cade covers of the ottoman and its cushions, supply all
the ornament, and are much too handsome to be hidden
by odds and ends of useless things. A few good oil-
paintings from the exhibitions in the Grosvenor Gallery
thirty years ago (the Burne Jones, not the Whistler side
of them) are on the walls. The only landscape is a Cecil
Lawson on the scale of a Rubens. There is a portrait of
Mrs Higgins as she was when she defied fashion in her
youth in one of the beautiful Rossettian costumes which,
when caricatured by people who did not understand, led
to the absurdities of popular estheticism in the eighteen-
seventies.

In the corner diagonally opposite the door Mrs Higgins, now over sixty and long past taking the trouble to

dress out of the fashion, sits writing at an elegantly simple writing-table with a bell button within reach of her hand. There is a Chippendale chair further back in the room between her and the window nearest her side. At the other side of the room, further forward, is an Elizabethan chair roughly carved in the taste of Inigo Jones. On the same side a piano in a decorated case. The corner between the fireplace and the window is occupied by a divan cushioned in Morris chintz.

It is between four and five in the afternoon.

The door is opened violently; and Higgins enters with his hat on.

MRS HIGGINS (*dismayed*): Henry! (*Scolding him*) What are you doing here today? It is my at-home day: you promised not to come. (*As he bends to kiss her, she takes his hat off, and presents it to him.*)

HIGGINS: Oh bother! (*He throws the hat down on the table.*)

MRS HIGGINS: Go home at once.

HIGGINS (*kissing her*): I know, mother. I came on purpose.

MRS HIGGINS: But you mustnt. I'm serious, Henry. You offend all my friends: they stop coming whenever they meet you.

HIGGINS: Nonsense! I know I have no small talk; but people dont mind. (*He sits on the settee.*)

MRS HIGGINS: Oh! dont they? Small talk indeed! What about your large talk? Really, dear, you mustnt stay.

HIGGINS: I must. Ive a job for you. A phonetic job.

MRS HIGGINS: No use, dear. I'm sorry; but I cant get round your vowels; and though I like to get pretty post-cards in your patent shorthand, I always have to read the copies in ordinary writing you so thoughtfully send me.

HIGGINS: Well, this isn't a phonetic job.

MRS HIGGINS: You said it was.

HIGGINS: Not your part of it. Ive picked up a girl.

MRS HIGGINS: Does that mean that some girl has picked you up?

HIGGINS: Not at all. I dont mean a love affair.

MRS HIGGINS: What a pity!

HIGGINS: Why?

MRS HIGGINS: Well, you never fall in love with anyone under forty-five. When will you discover that there are some rather nice-looking young women about?

HIGGINS: Oh, I cant be bothered with young women. My idea of a lovable woman is somebody as like you as possible. I shall never get into the way of seriously liking young women: some habits lie too deep to be changed. (*Rising abruptly and walking about, jingling his money and his keys in his trouser pockets*) Besides, theyre all idiots.

MRS HIGGINS: Do you know what you would do if you really loved me, Henry?

HIGGINS: Oh bother! What? Marry, I suppose.

MRS HIGGINS: No. Stop fidgeting and take your hands out of your pockets. (*With a gesture of despair, he obeys and sits down again.*) Thats a good boy. Now tell me about the girl.

HIGGINS: She's coming to see you.

MRS HIGGINS: I dont remember asking her.

HIGGINS: You didnt. *I* asked her. If youd known her you wouldnt have asked her.

MRS HIGGINS: Indeed! Why?

HIGGINS: Well, it's like this. She's a common flower girl. I picked her off the kerbstone.

MRS HIGGINS: And invited her to my at-home!

HIGGINS (*rising and coming to her to coax her*): Oh, thatll be all right. Ive taught her to speak properly; and she has strict orders as to her behavior. She's to keep to two subjects: the weather and everybody's health—Fine day and How do you do, you know—and not to let herself go on things in general. That will be safe.

MRS HIGGINS: Safe! To talk about our health! about our insides! perhaps about our outsides! How could you be so silly, Henry?

HIGGINS (*impatiently*): Well, she must talk about something. (*He controls himself and sits down again.*) Oh, she'll be all right: dont you fuss. Pickering is in it with me. Ive a sort of bet on that I'll pass her off as a duchess in six months. I started on her some months ago; and she's getting on like a house on fire. I shall win my bet. She has a quick ear; and she's been easier to teach than my middle-class pupils because she's had to learn a complete new language. She talks English almost as you talk French.

MRS HIGGINS: That satisfactory, at all events.

HIGGINS: Well, it is and it isnt.

MRS HIGGINS: What does that mean?

HIGGINS: You see, Ive got her pronunciation all right; but you have to consider not only how a girl pronounces, but what she pronounces; and that's where—

(*They are interrupted by the parlormaid, announcing guests.*)

THE PARLORMAID: Mrs and Miss Eynsford Hill. (*She withdraws.*)

HIGGINS: Oh Lord! (*He rises; snatches his hat from the table; and makes for the door; but before he reaches it his mother introduces him.*)

(*Mrs and Miss Eynsford Hill are the mother and daughter who sheltered from the rain in Covent Garden. The mother is well bred, quiet, and has the habitual anxiety of straitened means. The daughter has acquired a gay air of being very much at home in society: the bravado of genteel poverty.*)

MRS EYNSFORD HILL (*to Mrs Higgins*): How do you do? (*They shake hands.*)

MISS EYNSFORD HILL: How d'you do? (*She shakes.*)

MRS HIGGINS (*introducing*): My son Henry.

MRS EYNSFORD HILL: Your celebrated son! I have so longed to meet you, Professor Higgins.

HIGGINS (*glumly, making no movement in her direction*): Delighted. (*He backs against the piano and bows brusquely.*)

MISS EYNSFORD HILL (*going to him with confident familiarity*): How do you do?

HIGGINS (*staring at her*): Ive seen you before some-where. I havent the ghost of a notion where; but Ive heard your voice. (*Drearily*) It doesnt matter. Youd better sit down.

MRS HIGGINS: I'm sorry to say that my celebrated son has no manners. You mustnt mind him.

MISS EYNSFORD HILL (*gaily*): I dont. (*She sits in the Elizabethan chair.*)

MRS EYNSFORD HILL (*a little bewildered*): Not at all. (*She sits on the ottoman between her daughter and Mrs Higgins, who has turned her chair away from the writing-table.*)

HIGGINS: Oh, have I been rude? I didnt mean to be.

(*He goes to the central window, through which, with his back to the company, he contemplates the river and the flowers in Battersea Park on the opposite bank as if they were a frozen desert.*)

(*The parlormaid returns, ushering in Pickering.*)

THE PARLORMAID: Colonel Pickering. (*She withdraws.*)

PICKERING: How do you do, Mrs Higgins?

MRS HIGGINS: So glad youve come. Do you know Mrs Eynsford Hill—Miss Eynsford Hill? (*Exchange of bows. The Colonel brings the Chippendale chair a little forward between Mrs Hill and Mrs Higgins, and sits down.*)

PICKERING: Has Henry told you what weve come for?

HIGGINS (*over his shoulder*): We were interrupted: damn it!

MRS HIGGINS: Oh Henry, Henry, really!

MRS EYNSFORD HILL (*half rising*): Are we in the way?

MRS HIGGINS (*rising and making her sit down again*): No, no. You couldnt have come more fortunately: we want you to meet a friend of ours.

HIGGINS (*turning hopefully*): Yes, by George! We want two or three people. Youll do as well as anybody else.

(*The parlormaid returns, ushering Freddy.*)

THE PARLORMAID: Mr Eynsford Hill.

HIGGINS (*almost audibly, past endurance*): God of Heaven! another of them.

FREDDY (*shaking hands with Mrs Higgins*): Ahdedo?

MRS HIGGINS: Very good of you to come. (*Introducing*) Colonel Pickering.

FREDDY (*bowing*): Ahdedo?

MRS HIGGINS: I dont think you know my son, Professor Higgins.

FREDDY (*going to Higgins*): Ahdedo?

HIGGINS (*looking at him much as if he were a pickpocket*): I'll take my oath Ive met you before somewhere. Where was it?

FREDDY: I dont think so.

HIGGINS (*resignedly*): It dont matter, anyhow. Sit down. (*He shakes Freddy's hand, and almost slings him on to the ottoman with his face to the windows; then comes round to the other side of it.*)

HIGGINS: Well, here we are, anyhow! (*He sits down on the ottoman next Mrs Eynsford Hill on her left.*) And now what the devil are we going to talk about until Eliza comes?

MRS HIGGINS: Henry: you are the life and soul of the Royal Society's soirées; but really youre rather trying on more commonplace occasions.

HIGGINS: Am I? Very sorry. (*Beaming suddenly*) I suppose I am, you know. (*Uproariously*) Ha, ha!

MISS EYNSFORD HILL (*who considers Higgins quite eligible matrimonially*): I sympathize. *I* havnt any small talk. If people would only be frank and say what they really think!

HIGGINS (*relapsing into gloom*): Lord forbid!

MRS EYNSFORD HILL (*taking up her daughter's cue*): But why?

HIGGINS: What they think they ought to think is bad enough Lord knows; but what they really think would break up the whole show. Do you suppose it would be really agreeable if I were to come out now with what *I* really think?

MISS EYNSFORD HILL (*gaily*): Is it so very cynical?

HIGGINS: Cynical! Who the dickens said it was cynical? I mean it wouldnt be decent.

MISS EYNSFORD HILL (*seriously*): Oh! I'm sure you dont mean that, Mr Higgins.

HIGGINS: You see, we're all savages, more or less. We're supposed to be civilized and cultured—to know all about poetry and philosophy and art and science, and so on; but how many of us know even the meanings of these names? (*To Miss Hill*) What do you know of poetry? (*To Mrs Hill*) What do you know of science? (*Indicating Freddy*) What does he know of art or science or anything else? What the devil do you imagine I know of philosophy?

MRS HIGGINS (*warningly*): Or of manners, Henry?

THE PARLORMAID (*opening the door*): Miss Doolittle. (*She withdraws.*)

HIGGINS (*rising hastily and running to Mrs Higgins*): Here she is, mother. (*He stands on tiptoe and makes signs over his mother's head to Eliza to indicate to her which lady is her hostess.*)

(*Eliza, who is exquisitely dressed, produces an impression of such remarkable distinction and beauty as she enters that they all rise, quite fluttered. Guided by Higgins's signals, she comes to Mrs Higgins with studied grace.*)

LIZA (*speaking with pedantic correctness of pronunciation and great beauty of tone*): How do you do, Mrs Higgins? (*She gasps slightly in making sure of the H in Higgins, but is quite successful.*) Mr Higgins told me I might come.

MRS HIGGINS (*cordially*): Quite right: I'm very glad indeed to see you.

PICKERING: How do you do, Miss Doolittle?

LIZA (*shaking hands with him*): Colonel Pickering, is it not?

MRS EYNSFORD HILL: I feel sure we have met before, Miss Doolittle. I remember your eyes.

LIZA: How do you do? (*She sits down on the ottoman gracefully in the place just left vacant by Higgins.*)

MRS EYNSFORD HILL (*introducing*): My daughter Clara.

LIZA: How do you do?

CLARA (*impulsively*): How do you do? (*She sits down on the ottoman beside Eliza, devouring her with her eyes.*)

FREDDY (*coming to their side of the ottoman*): Ive certainly had the pleasure.

MRS EYNSFORD HILL (*introducing*): My son Freddy.

LIZA: How do you do?

(*Freddy bows and sits down in the Elizabethan chair, infatuated.*)

HIGGINS (*suddenly*): By George, yes: it all comes back to me! (*They stare at him.*) Covent Garden! (*Lamentably*) What a damned thing!

MRS HIGGINS: Henry, please! (*He is about to sit on the edge of the table.*) Dont sit on my writing-table: youll break it.

HIGGINS (*sulkily*): Sorry.

(*He goes to the divan, stumbling into the fender and over the fire-irons on his way; extricating himself with muttered imprecations; and finishing his disastrous journey by throwing himself so impatiently on the divan that he almost breaks it. Mrs Higgins looks at him, but controls herself and says nothing.*)

(*A long and painful pause ensues.*)

MRS HIGGINS (*at last, conversationally*): Will it rain, do you think?

LIZA: The shallow depression in the west of these islands is likely to move slowly in an easterly direction. There are no indications of any great change in the barometrical situation.

FREDDY: Ha! ha! how awfully funny!

LIZA: What is wrong with that, young man? I bet I got it right.

FREDDY: Killing!

MRS EYNSFORD HILL: I'm sure I hope it wont turn cold. There so much influenza about. It runs right through our whole family regularly every spring.

LIZA (*darkly*): My aunt died of influenza: so they said.

MRS EYNSFORD HILL (*clicks her tongue sympathetically*): ! ! !

LIZA (*in the same tragic tone*): But it's my belief they done the old woman in.

MRS HIGGINS (*puzzled*): Done her in?

LIZA: Y-e-e-e-es, Lord love you! Why should she die of influenza? She come through diphtheria right enough the year before. I saw her with my own eyes. Fairly blue with it, she was. They all thought she was dead; but my father he kept ladling gin down her throat til she came to so sudden that she bit the bowl off the spoon.

MRS EYNSFORD HILL (*startled*): Dear me!

LIZA (*piling up the indictment*): What call would a woman with that strength in her have to die of influenza? What become of her new straw hat that should have come to me? Somebody pinched it; and what I say is, them as pinched it done her in.

MRS EYNSFORD HILL: What does doing her in mean?

HIGGINS (*hastily*): Oh, thats the new small talk. To do a person in means to kill them.

MRS EYNSFORD HILL (*to Eliza, horrified*): You surely dont believe that your aunt was killed?

LIZA: Do I not! Them she lived with would have killed her for a hat-pin, let alone a hat.

MRS EYNSFORD HILL: But it cant have been right for your father to pour spirits down her throat like that. It might have killed her.

LIZA: Not her. Gin was mother's milk to her. Besides, he'd poured so much down his own throat that he knew the good of it.

MRS EYNSFORD HILL: Do you mean that he drank?

LIZA: Drank! My word! Something chronic.

MRS EYNSFORD HILL: How dreadful for you!

LIZA: Not a bit. It never did him no harm what I could see. But then he did not keep it up regular. (*Cheerfully*) On the burst, as you might say, from time to time. And always more agreeable when he had a drop in. When he was out of work, my mother used to give him fourpence and tell him to go out and not come back until he'd drunk himself cheerful and loving-like. Theres lots of women has to make their husbands drunk to make them fit to live with. (*Now quite at her ease*) You see, it's like this. If a man has a bit of a conscience, it always takes him when he's sober; and then it makes him low-spirited.

A drop of booze just takes that off and makes him happy. (*To Freddy, who is in convulsions of suppressed laughter*) Here! what are you sniggering at?

FREDDY: The new small talk. You do it so awfully well.

LIZA: If I was doing it proper, what was you laughing at? (*To Higgins*) Have I said anything I oughtnt?

MRS HIGGINS (*interposing*): Not at all, Miss Doolittle.

LIZA: Well, thats a mercy, anyhow. (*Expansively*) What I always say is—

HIGGINS (*rising and looking at his watch*): Ahem!

LIZA (*looking round at him; taking the hint; and rising*): Well: I must go. (*They all rise. Freddy goes to the door.*) So pleased to have met you. Goodbye. (*She shakes hands with Mrs Higgins.*)

MRS HIGGINS: Goodbye.

LIZA: Goodbye, Colonel Pickering.

PICKERING: Goodbye, Miss Doolittle. (*They shake hands.*)

LIZA (*nodding to the others*): Goodbye, all.

FREDDY (*opening the door for her*): Are you walking across the Park, Miss Doolittle? If so—

LIZA (*with perfectly elegant diction*): Walk! Not bloody likely. (*Sensation*) I am going in a taxi. (*She goes out.*)

(*Pickering gasps and sits down. Freddy goes out on the balcony to catch another glimpse of Eliza.*)

MRS EYNSFORD HILL (*suffering from shock*): Well, I really cant get used to the new ways.

CLARA (*throwing herself discontentedly into the Elizabethan chair*): Oh, it's all right, mamma, quite right. People will think we never go anywhere or see anybody if you are so old-fashioned.

MRS EYNSFORD HILL: I daresay I am very old-fashioned; but I do hope you wont begin using that expression, Clara. I have got accustomed to hear you talking about men as rotters, and calling everything filthy and beastly; though I do think it horrible and unladylike. But this last is really too much. Dont you think so, Colonel Pickering?

PICKERING: Dont ask me. Ive been away in India for several years; and manners have changed so much that

I sometimes dont know whether I'm at a respectable dinner-table or in a ship's forecastle.

CLARA: It's all a matter of habit. Theres no right or wrong in it. Nobody means anything by it. And it's so quaint, and gives such a smart emphasis to things that are not in themselves very witty. I find the new small talk delightful and quite innocent.

MRS EYNSFORD HILL (*rising*): Well, after that, I think it's time for us to go.

(*Pickering and Higgins rise.*)

CLARA (*rising*): Oh yes: we have three at-homes to go to still. Goodbye, Mrs Higgins. Goodbye, Colonel Pickering. Goodbye, Professor Higgins.

HIGGINS (*coming grimly at her from the divan, and accompanying her to the door*): Goodbye. Be sure you try on that small talk at the three at-homes. Dont be nervous about it. Pitch it in strong.

CLARA (*all smiles*): I will. Goodbye. Such nonsense, all this early Victorian prudery!

HIGGINS (*tempting her*): Such damned nonsense!

CLARA: Such bloody nonsense!

MRS EYNSFORD HILL (*convulsively*): Clara!

CLARA: Ha! ha! (*She goes out radiant, conscious of being thoroughly up to date, and is heard descending the stairs in a stream of silvery laughter.*)

FREDDY (*to the heavens at large*): Well, I ask you— (*He gives it up, and comes to Mrs Higgins.*) Goodbye.

MRS HIGGINS (*shaking hands*): Goodbye. Would you like to meet Miss Doolittle again?

FREDDY (*eagerly*): Yes, I should, most awfully.

MRS HIGGINS: Well, you know my days.

FREDDY: Yes, thanks awfully. Goodbye. (*He goes out.*)

MRS EYNSFORD HILL: Goodbye, Mr Higgins.

HIGGINS: Goodbye. Goodbye.

MRS EYNSFORD HILL (*to Pickering*): It's no use. I shall never be able to bring myself to use that word.

PICKERING: Dont. It's not compulsory, you know. Youll get on quite well without it.

MRS EYNSFORD HILL: Only, Clara is so down on me if I am not positively reeking with the latest slang. Goodbye.

PICKERING: Goodbye. (*they shake hands.*)

MRS EYNSFORD HILL (*to Mrs Higgins*): You mustnt mind Clara. (*Pickering, catching from her lowered tone that this is not meant for him to hear, discreetly joins Higgins at the window.*) We're so poor! and she gets so few parties, poor child! She doesnt quite know. (*Mrs Higgins, seeing that her eyes are moist, takes her hand sympathetically and goes with her to the door.*) But the boy is nice. Dont you think so?

MRS HIGGINS: Oh, quite nice. I shall always be delighted to see him.

MRS EYNSFORD HILL: Thank you, dear. Goodbye. (*She goes out.*)

HIGGINS (*eagerly*): Well? Is Eliza presentable? (*He swoops on his mother and drags her to the ottoman, where she sits down in Eliza's place with her son on her left.*)

(*Pickering returns to his chair on her right.*)

MRS HIGGINS: You silly boy, of course she's not presentable. She's a triumph of your art and of her dressmaker's; but if you suppose for a moment that she doesnt give herself away in every sentence she utters, you must be perfectly cracked about her.

PICKERING: But dont you think something might be done? I mean something to eliminate the sanguinary element from her conversation.

MRS HIGGINS: Not as long as she is in Henry's hands.

HIGGINS (*aggrieved*): Do you mean that my language is improper?

MRS HIGGINS: No, dearest: it would be quite proper— say on a canal barge; but it would not be proper for her at a garden party.

HIGGINS (*deeply injured*): Well I must say—

PICKERING (*interrupting him*): Come, Higgins: you must learn to know yourself. I havnt heard such language as yours since we used to review the volunteers in Hyde Park twenty years ago.

HIGGINS (*sulkily*): Oh, well, if you say so, I suppose I dont always talk like a bishop.

MRS HIGGINS (*quieting Henry with a touch*): Colonel Pickering: will you tell me what is the exact state of things in Wimpole Street?

PICKERING (*cheerfully: as if this completely changed the subject*): Well, I have come to live there with Henry. We work together at my Indian Dialects; and we think it more convenient—

MRS HIGGINS: Quite so. I know all about that: it's an excellent arrangement. But where does this girl live?

HIGGINS: With us, of course. Where should she live?

MRS HIGGINS: But on what terms? Is she a servant? If not, what is she?

PICKERING (*slowly*): I think I know what you mean, Mrs Higgins.

HIGGINS: Well, dash me if *I* do! Ive had to work at the girl every day for months to get her to her present pitch. Besides, she's useful. She knows where my things are, and remembers my appointments and so forth.

MRS HIGGINS: How does your housekeeper get on with her?

HIGGINS: Mrs Pearce? Oh, she's jolly glad to get so much taken off her hands; for before Eliza came, she used to have to find things and remind me of my appointments. But she's got some silly bee in her bonnet about Eliza. She keeps saying "You dont think, sir": doesnt she, Pick?

PICKERING: Yes: thats the formula. "You dont think, sir." Thats the end of every conversation about Eliza.

HIGGINS: As if I ever stop thinking about the girl and her confounded vowels and consonants. I'm worn out, thinking about her, and watching her lips and her teeth and her tongue, not to mention her soul, which is the quaintest of the lot.

MRS HIGGINS: You certainly are a pretty pair of babies, playing with your live doll.

HIGGINS: Playing! The hardest job I ever tackled: make

no mistake about that, mother. But you have no idea how frightfully interesting it is to take a human being and change her into a quite different human being by creating a new speech for her. It's filling up the deepest gulf that separates class from class and soul from soul.

PICKERING (*drawing his chair closer to Mrs Higgins and bending over to her eagerly*): Yes: it's enormously interesting. I assure you, Mrs Higgins, we take Eliza very seriously. Every week—every day almost—there is some new change. (*Closer again*) We keep records of every stage—dozens of gramophone disks and photographs—

HIGGINS (*assailing her at the other ear*): Yes, by George: it's the most absorbing experiment I ever tackled. She regularly fills our lives up: doesnt she, Pick?

PICKERING: We're always talking Eliza.

HIGGINS: Teaching Eliza.

PICKERING: Dressing Eliza.

MRS HIGGINS: What!

HIGGINS: Inventing new Elizas.

HIGGINS	(*speaking together*)	You know, she has the most extraordinary quickness of ear:
PICKERING		I assure you, my dear Mrs Higgins, that girl

HIGGINS		just like a parrot. Ive tried her with every
PICKERING		is a genius. She can play the piano quite beautifully.

HIGGINS		possible sort of sound that a human being can make
PICKERING		We have taken her to classical concerts and to music

HIGGINS		Continental dialects, African dialects, Hottentot
PICKERING		halls; and it's all the same to her: she plays everything

| HIGGINS | | clicks, things it took me years to get hold of; and |
| PICKERING | (*speaking together*) | she hears right off when she comes home, whether it's |

| HIGGINS | | she picks them up like a shot, right away, as if she had |
| PICKERING | | Beethoven and Brahms or Lehar and Lionel Monckton; |

| HIGGINS | | been at it all her life. |
| PICKERING | | though six months ago, she'd never as much as touched a piano— |

MRS HIGGINS (*putting her fingers in her ears, as they are by this time shouting one another down with an intolerable noise*): Sh-sh-sh—sh! (*They stop.*)

PICKERING: I beg your pardon. (*He draws his chair back apologetically.*)

HIGGINS: Sorry. When Pickering starts shouting nobody can get a word in edgeways.

MRS HIGGINS: Be quiet, Henry. Colonel Pickering: dont you realize that when Eliza walked into Wimpole Street, something walked in with her?

PICKERING: Her father did. But Henry soon got rid of him.

MRS HIGGINS: It would have been more to the point if her mother had. But as her mother didnt something else did.

PICKERING: But what?

MRS HIGGINS (*unconsciously dating herself by the word*): A problem.

PICKERING: Oh, I see. The problem of how to pass her off as a lady.

HIGGINS: I'll solve that problem. Ive half solved it already.

MRS HIGGINS: No, you two infinitely stupid male creatures: the problem of what is to be done with her afterwards.

HIGGINS: I dont see anything in that. She can go her own way, with all the advantages I have given her.

MRS HIGGINS: The advantages of that poor woman who was here just now! The manners and habits that disqualify a fine lady from earning her own living without giving her a fine lady's income! Is that what you mean?

PICKERING (*indulgently, being rather bored*): Oh, that will be all right, Mrs Higgins. (*He rises to go.*)

HIGGINS (*rising also*): We'll find her some light employment.

PICKERING: She's happy enough. Dont you worry about her. Goodbye. (*He shakes hands as if he were consoling a frightened child, and makes for the door.*)

HIGGINS: Anyhow, theres no good bothering now. The thing's done. Goodbye, mother. (*He kisses her, and follows Pickering.*)

PICKERING (*turning for a final consolation*): There are plenty of openings. We'll do whats right. Goodbye.

HIGGINS (*to Pickering as they go out together*): Lets take her to the Shakespear exhibition at Earls Court.

PICKERING: Yes: lets. Her remarks will be delicious.

HIGGINS: She'll mimic all the people for us when we get home.

PICKERING: Ripping. (*Both are heard laughing as they go downstairs.*)

MRS HIGGINS (*rises with an impatient bounce, and returns to her work at the writing-table. She sweeps a litter of disarranged papers out of her way; snatches a sheet of paper from her stationery case; and tries resolutely to write. At the third line she gives it up; flings down her pen; grips the table angrily and exclaims*): Oh, men! men!! men!!!

* * *

Clearly Eliza will not pass as a duchess yet; and Higgins's bet remains unwon. But the six months are not yet exhausted; and just in time Eliza does actually pass as a princess. For a glimpse of how she did it imagine an Embassy in London one summer evening after dark. The hall door has an awning and a carpet across the sidewalk to the kerb, because a grand reception is in progress. A small crowd is lined up to see the guests arrive.

A Rolls-Royce car drives up. Pickering in evening dress, with medals and orders, alights, and hands out Eliza, in opera cloak, evening dress, diamonds, fan, flowers and all accessories. Higgins follows. The car drives off; and the three go up the steps and into the house, the door opening for them as they approach.

Inside the house they find themselves in a spacious hall from which the grand staircase rises. On the left are the arrangements for the gentlemen's cloaks. The male guests are depositing their hats and wraps there.

On the right is a door leading to the ladies' cloakroom. Ladies are going in cloaked and coming out in splendor. Pickering whispers to Eliza and points out the ladies' room. She goes into it. Higgins and Pickering take off their overcoats and take tickets for them from the attendant.

One of the guests, occupied in the same way, has his back turned. Having taken his ticket, he turns round and reveals himself as an important-looking young man with an astonishingly hairy face. He has an enormous moustache, flowing out into luxuriant whiskers. Waves of hair cluster on his brow. His hair is cropped closely at the back, and glows with oil. Otherwise he is very smart. He wears several worthless orders. He is evidently a foreigner, guessable as a whiskered Pandour from Hungary; but in spite of the ferocity of his moustache he is amiable and genially voluble.

Recognizing Higgins, he flings his arms wide apart and approaches him enthusiastically.

WHISKERS: Maestro, maestro (*he embraces Higgins and kisses him on both cheeks*). You remember me?

HIGGINS: No I dont. Who the devil are you?

WHISKERS: I am your pupil: your first pupil, your best and greatest pupil. I am little Nepommuck, the marvellous boy. I have made your name famous throughout Europe. You teach me phonetic. You cannot forget ME.

HIGGINS: Why dont you shave?

NEPOMMUCK: I have not your imposing appearance,

your chin, your brow. Nobody notice me when I shave. Now I am famous: they call me Hairy Faced Dick.

HIGGINS: And what are you doing here among all these swells?

NEPOMMUCK: I am interpreter. I speak 32 languages. I am indispensable at these international parties. You are great cockney specialist: you place a man anywhere in London the moment he open his mouth. I place any man in Europe.

(*A footman hurries down the grand staircase and comes to Nepommuck.*)

FOOTMAN: You are wanted upstairs. Her Excellency cannot understand the Greek gentleman.

NEPOMMUCK: Thank you, yes, immediately.

(*The footman goes and is lost in the crowd.*)

NEPOMMUCK (*to Higgins*): This Greek diplomatist pretends he cannot speak nor understand English. He cannot deceive me. He is the son of a Clerkenwell watchmaker. He speaks English so villainously that he dare not utter a word of it without betraying his origin. I help him to pretend; but I make him pay through the nose. I make them all pay. Ha Ha! (*He hurries upstairs.*)

PICKERING: Is this fellow really an expert? Can he find out Eliza and blackmail her?

HIGGINS: We shall see. If he finds her out I lose my bet.

(*Eliza comes from the cloakroom and joins them.*)

PICKERING: Well, Eliza, now for it. Are you ready?

LIZA: Are you nervous, Colonel?

PICKERING: Frightfully. I feel exactly as I felt before my first battle. It's the first time that frightens.

LIZA: It is not the first time for me, Colonel. I have done this fifty times—hundreds of times—in my little piggery in Angel Court in my day-dreams. I am in a dream now. Promise me not to let Professor Higgins wake me; for if he does I shall forget everything and talk as I used to in Drury Lane.

PICKERING: Not a word, Higgins. (*To Eliza*) Now, ready?

LIZA: Ready.

PICKERING: Go.

(*They mount the stairs, Higgins last. Pickering whispers to the footman on the first landing.*)

FIRST LANDING FOOTMAN: Miss Doolittle, Colonel Pickering, Professor Higgins.

SECOND LANDING FOOTMAN: Miss Doolittle, Colonel Pickering, Professor Higgins.

(*At the top of the staircase the Ambassador and his wife, with Nepommuck at her elbow, are receiving.*)

HOSTESS (*taking Eliza's hand*): How d'ye do?

HOST (*same play*): How d'ye do? How d'ye do, Pickering?

LIZA (*with a beautiful gravity that awes her hostess*): How do you do? (*She passes on to the drawing room.*)

HOSTESS: Is that your adopted daughter, Colonel Pickering? She will make a sensation.

PICKERING: Most kind of you to invite her for me. (*He passes on.*)

HOSTESS (*to Nepommuck*): Find out all about her.

NEPOMMUCK (*bowing*): Excellency— (*He goes into the crowd.*)

HOST: How d'ye do, Higgins? You have a rival here tonight. He introduced himself as your pupil. Is he any good?

HIGGINS: He can learn a language in a fortnight— knows dozens of them. A sure mark of a fool. As a phonetician, no good whatever.

HOSTESS: How d'ye do, Professor?

HIGGINS: How do you do? Fearful bore for you this sort of thing. Forgive my part in it. (*He passes on.*)

In the drawing room and its suite of salons the reception is in full swing. Eliza passes through. She is so intent on her ordeal that she walks like a somnambulist in a desert instead of a débutante in a fashionable crowd. They stop talking to look at her, admiring her dress, her jewels, and her strangely attractive self. Some of the younger ones at the back stand on their chairs to see.

The Host and Hostess come in from the staircase and

mingle with their guests. Higgins, gloomy and contemp-
tuous of the whole business, comes into the group where
they are chatting.

HOSTESS: Ah, here is Professor Higgins: he will tell us.
Tell us all about the wonderful young lady, Professor.

HIGGINS (*almost morosely*): What wonderful young
lady?

HOSTESS: You know very well. They tell me there has
been nothing like her in London since people stood on
their chairs to look at Mrs Langtry.

(*Nepommuck joins the group, full of news.*)

HOSTESS: Ah, here you are at last, Nepommuck. Have
you found out all about the Doolittle lady?

NEPOMMUCK: I have found out all about her. She is
a fraud.

HOSTESS: A fraud! Oh no.

NEPOMMUCK: YES, yes. She cannot deceive me. Her
name cannot be Doolittle.

HIGGINS: Why?

NEPOMMUCK: Because Doolittle is an English name.
And she is not English.

HOSTESS: Oh, nonsense! She speaks English perfectly.

NEPOMMUCK: Too perfectly. Can you shew me any English woman who speaks English as it should be spoken?
Only foreigners who have been taught to speak it speak
it well.

HOSTESS: Certainly she terrified me by the way she
said How d'ye do. I had a schoolmistress who talked
like that; and I was mortally afraid of her. But if she is
not English what is she?

NEPOMMUCK: Hungarian.

ALL THE REST: Hungarian!

NEPOMMUCK: Hungarian. And of royal blood. I am
Hungarian. My blood is royal.

HIGGINS: Did you speak to her in Hungarian?

NEPOMMUCK: I did. She was very clever. She said
"Please speak to me in English! I do not understand
French." French! She pretends not to know the differ-

ence between Hungarian and French. Impossible: she knows both.

HIGGINS: And the blood royal? How did you find that out?

NEPOMMUCK: Instinct, maestro, instinct. Only the Magyar races can produce that air of the divine right, those resolute eyes. She is a princess.

HOST: What do you say, Professor?

HIGGINS: I say an ordinary London girl out of the gutter and taught to speak by an expert. I place her in Drury Lane.

NEPOMMUCK: Ha ha ha! Oh, maestro, maestro, you are mad on the subject of cockney dialects. The London gutter is the whole world for you.

HIGGINS (*to the Hostess*): What does your Excellency say?

HOSTESS: Oh, of course I agree with Nepommuck. She must be a princess at least.

HOST: Not necessarily legitimate, of course. Morganatic perhaps. But that is undoubtedly her class.

HIGGINS: I stick to my opinion.

HOSTESS: Oh, you are incorrigible.

(*The group breaks up, leaving Higgins isolated. Pickering joins him.*)

PICKERING: Where is Eliza? We must keep an eye on her.

(*Eliza joins them.*)

LIZA: I dont think I can bear much more. The people all stare so at me. An old lady has just told me that I speak exactly like Queen Victoria. I am sorry if I have lost your bet. I have done my best; but nothing can make me the same as these people.

PICKERING: You have not lost it, my dear. You have won it ten times over.

HIGGINS: Let us get out of this. I have had enough of chattering to these fools.

PICKERING: Eliza is tired; and I am hungry. Let us clear out and have supper somewhere.

ACT FOUR

The Wimpole Street laboratory. Midnight. Nobody in the room. The clock on the mantel-piece strikes twelve. The fire is not alight: it is a summer night.

Presently Higgins and Pickering are heard on the stairs.

HIGGINS (*calling down to Pickering*): I say, Pick: lock up, will you? I shant be going out again.

PICKERING: Right. Can Mrs Pearce go to bed? We dont want anything more, do we?

HIGGINS: Lord, no!

(*Eliza opens the door and is seen on the lighted landing in all the finery in which she has just won Higgins's bet for him. She comes to the hearth, and switches on the electric lights there. She is tired: her pallor contrasts strongly with her dark eyes and hair; and her expression is almost tragic. She takes off her cloak; puts her fan and gloves on the piano; and sits down on the bench, brooding and silent. Higgins, in evening dress, with overcoat and hat, comes in, carrying a smoking jacket which he has picked up downstairs. He takes off the hat and overcoat; throws them carelessly on the newspaper stand; disposes of his coat in the same way; puts on the smoking jacket; and throws himself wearily into the easy-chair at the hearth. Pickering, similarly attired, comes in. He also takes off his hat and overcoat, and is about to throw them on Higgins's when he hesitates.*)

PICKERING: I say: Mrs Pearce will row if we leave these things lying about in the drawing room.

HIGGINS: Oh, chuck them over the bannisters into the

hall. She'll find them there in the morning and put them away all right. She'll think we were drunk.

PICKERING: We are, slightly. Are there any letters?

HIGGINS: I didnt look. (*Pickering takes the overcoats and hats and goes downstairs. Higgins begins half singing half yawning an air from* La Fanciulla del Golden West. *Suddenly he stops and exclaims*) I wonder where the devil my slippers are!

(*Eliza looks at him darkly; then rises suddenly and leaves the room.*

(*Higgins yawns again, and resumes his song.*

(*Pickering returns, with the contents of the letter-box in his hand.*)

PICKERING: Only circulars, and this coroneted billet-doux for you. (*He throws the circulars into the fender, and posts himself on the hearthrug, with his back to the grate.*)

HIGGINS (*glancing at the billet-doux*): Money-lender. (*He throws the letter after the circulars.*)

(*Eliza returns with a pair of large down-at-heel slippers. She places them on the carpet before Higgins, and sits as before without a word.*)

HIGGINS (*yawning again*): Oh Lord! What an evening! What a crew! What a silly tomfoolery! (*He raises his shoe to unlace it, and catches sight of the slippers. He stops unlacing and looks at them as if they had appeared there of their own accord.*) Oh! theyre there, are they?

PICKERING (*stretching himself*): Well, I feel a bit tired. It's been a long day. The garden party, a dinner party, and the reception! Rather too much of a good thing. But youve won your bet, Higgins. Eliza did the trick, and something to spare, eh?

HIGGINS (*fervently*): Thank God it's over!

(*Eliza flinches violently; but they take no notice of her; and she recovers herself and sits stonily as before.*)

PICKERING: Were you nervous at the garden party? *I* was. Eliza didnt seem a bit nervous.

HIGGINS: Oh, she wasnt nervous. I knew she'd be all right. No: it's the strain of putting the job through all these months that has told on me. It was interesting enough at first, while we were at the phonetics; but after that I got deadly sick of it. If I hadnt backed myself to do it I should have chucked the whole thing up two months ago. It was a silly notion: the whole thing has been a bore.

PICKERING: Oh come! the garden party was frightfully exciting. My heart began beating like anything.

HIGGINS: Yes, for the first three minutes. But when I saw we were going to win hands down, I felt like a bear in a cage, hanging about doing nothing. The dinner was worse: sitting gorging there for over an hour, with nobody but a damned fool of a fashionable woman to talk to! I tell you, Pickering, never again for me. No more artificial duchesses. The whole thing has been simple purgatory.

PICKERING: Youve never been broken in properly to the social routine. (*Strolling over to the piano*) I rather enjoy dipping into it occasionally myself: it makes me feel young again. Anyhow, it was a great success: an immense success. I was quite frightened once or twice because Eliza was doing it so well. You see, lots of the real people cant do it at all: theyre such fools that they think style comes by nature to people in their position; and so they never learn. Theres always something professional about doing a thing superlatively well.

HIGGINS: Yes: thats what drives me mad: the silly people dont know their own silly business. (*Rising*) However, it's over and done with; and now I can go to bed at last without dreading tomorrow.

(*Eliza's beauty becomes murderous.*)

PICKERING: I think I shall turn in too. Still, it's been a great occasion: a triumph for you. Goodnight. (*He goes.*)

HIGGINS (*following him*): Goodnight. (*Over his shoulder, at the door*) Put out the lights, Eliza; and tell Mrs Pearce not to make coffee for me in the morning: I'll take tea. (*He goes out.*)

(*Eliza tries to control herself and feel indifferent as she rises and walks across to the hearth to switch off the*

*lights. By the time she gets there she is on the point of
screaming. She sits down in Higgins's chair and holds on
hard to the arms. Finally she gives way and flings herself
furiously on the floor, raging.*)

HIGGINS (*in despairing wrath outside*): What the devil
have I done with my slippers? (*He appears at the door.*)

LIZA (*snatching up the slippers, and hurling them at
him one after the other with all her force*): There are
your slippers. And there. Take your slippers; and may
you never have a day's luck with them!

HIGGINS (*astounded*): What on earth—! (*He comes to
her.*) Whats the matter? Get up. (*He pulls her up.*) Anything wrong?

LIZA (*breathless*): Nothing wrong—with you. Ive won
your bet for you, havnt I? Thats enough for you. *I* dont
matter, I suppose.

HIGGINS: You won my bet! You! Presumptuous insect!
I won it. What did you throw those slippers at me for?

LIZA: Because I wanted to smash your face. I'd like
to kill you, you selfish brute. Why didnt you leave me
where you picked me out of—in the gutter? You thank
God it's all over, and that now you can throw me back
again there, do you? (*She crisps her fingers frantically.*)

HIGGINS (*looking at her in cool wonder*): The creature
is nervous, after all.

LIZA (*gives a suffocated scream of fury, and instinctively darts her nails at his face*): !!

HIGGINS (*catching her wrists*): Ah! would you? Claws
in, you cat. How dare you shew your temper to me?
Sit down and be quiet. (*He throws her roughly into the
easy-chair.*)

LIZA (*crushed by superior strength and weight*): Whats
to become of me? Whats to become of me?

HIGGINS: How the devil do I know whats to become
of you? What does it matter what becomes of you?

LIZA: You dont care. I know you dont care. You
wouldnt care if I was dead. I'm nothing to you—not so
much as them slippers.

HIGGINS (*thundering*): Those slippers.

LIZA (*with bitter submission*): Those slippers. I didnt think it made any difference now.

(*A pause. Eliza hopeless and crushed. Higgins a little uneasy.*)

HIGGINS (*in his loftiest manner*): Why have you begun going on like this? May I ask whether you complain of your treatment here?

LIZA: No.

HIGGINS: Has anybody behaved badly to you? Colonel Pickering? Mrs Pearce? Any of the servants?

LIZA: No.

HIGGINS: I presume you dont pretend that *I* have treated you badly?

LIZA: No.

HIGGINS: I am glad to hear it. (*He moderates his tone.*) Perhaps youre tired after the strain of the day. Will you have a glass of champagne? (*He moves towards the door.*)

LIZA: No. (*Recollecting her manners*) Thank you.

HIGGINS (*good-humored again*): This has been coming on you for some days. I suppose it was natural for you to be anxious about the garden party. But thats all over now. (*He pats her kindly on the shoulder. She writhes.*) Theres nothing more to worry about.

LIZA: No. Nothing more for you to worry about. (*She suddenly rises and gets away from him by going to the piano bench, where she sits and hides her face.*) Oh God! I wish I was dead.

HIGGINS (*staring after her in sincere surprise*): Why? In heaven's name, why? (*Reasonably, going to her*) Listen to me, Eliza. All this irritation is purely subjective.

LIZA: I dont understand. I'm too ignorant.

HIGGINS: It's only imagination. Low spirits and nothing else. Nobody's hurting you. Nothing's wrong. You go to bed like a good girl and sleep it off. Have a little cry and say your prayers: that will make you comfortable.

LIZA: I heard your prayers. "Thank God it's all over!"

HIGGINS (*impatiently*): Well, dont you thank God it's all over? Now you are free and can do what you like.

LIZA (*pulling herself together in desperation*): What am I fit for? What have you left me fit for? Where am I to go? What am I to do? Whats to become of me?

HIGGINS (*enlightened, but not at all impressed*): Oh, thats whats worrying you, is it? (*He thrusts his hands into his pockets, and walks about in his usual manner, rattling the contents of his pockets, as if condescending to a trivial subject out of pure kindness.*) I shouldnt bother about it if I were you. I should imagine you wont have much difficulty in settling yourself somewhere or other, though I hadnt quite realized that you were going away. (*She looks quickly at him: he does not look at her, but examines the dessert stand on the piano and decides that he will eat an apple.*) You might marry, you know. (*He bites a large piece out of the apple and munches it noisily.*) You see, Eliza, all men are not confirmed old bachelors like me and the Colonel. Most men are the marrying sort (poor devils!); and youre not bad-looking: it's quite a pleasure to look at you sometimes—not now, of course, because youre crying and looking as ugly as the very devil; but when youre all right and quite yourself, youre what I should call attractive. That is, to the people in the marrying line, you understand. You go to bed and have a good nice rest; and then get up and look at yourself in the glass; and you wont feel so cheap.

(*Eliza again looks at him, speechless, and does not stir. (The look is quite lost on him: he eats his apple with a dreamy expression of happiness, as it is quite a good one.*)

HIGGINS (*a genial afterthought occurring to him*): I daresay my mother could find some chap or other who would do very well.

LIZA: We were above that at the corner of Tottenham Court Road.

HIGGINS (*waking up*): What do you mean?

LIZA: I sold flowers. I didnt sell myself. Now youve made a lady of me I'm not fit to sell anything else. I wish youd left me where you found me.

HIGGINS (*slinging the core of the apple decisively into the grate*): Tosh, Eliza. Dont you insult human relations by dragging all this cant about buying and selling into it. You neednt marry the fellow if you dont like him.

LIZA: What else am I to do?

HIGGINS: Oh, lots of things. What about your old idea of a florist's shop? Pickering could set you up in one: he has lots of money. (*Chuckling*) He'll have to pay for all those togs you have been wearing today; and that, with the hire of the jewellery, will make a big hole in two hundred pounds. Why, six months ago you would have thought it the millennium to have a flower shop of your own. Come! youll be all right. I must clear off to bed: I'm devilish sleepy. By the way, I came down for something: I forget what it was.

LIZA: Your slippers.

HIGGINS: Oh yes, of course. You shied them at me. (*He picks them up, and is going out when she rises and speaks to him.*)

LIZA: Before you go, sir—

HIGGINS (*dropping the slippers in his surprise at her calling him Sir*): Eh?

LIZA: Do my clothes belong to me or to Colonel Pickering?

HIGGINS (*coming back into the room as if her question were the very climax of unreason*): What the devil use would they be to Pickering?

LIZA: He might want them for the next girl you pick up to experiment on.

HIGGINS (*shocked and hurt*): Is that the way you feel towards us?

LIZA: I dont want to hear anything more about that. All I want to know is whether anything belongs to me. My own clothes were burnt.

HIGGINS: But what does it matter? Why need you start bothering about that in the middle of the night?

LIZA: I want to know what I may take away with me. I dont want to be accused of stealing.

HIGGINS (*now deeply wounded*): Stealing! You shouldnt have said that, Eliza. That shews a want of feeling.

LIZA: I'm sorry. I'm only a common ignorant girl; and in my station I have to be careful. There cant be any feelings between the like of you and the like of me. Please will you tell me what belongs to me and what doesnt?

HIGGINS (*very sulky*): You may take the whole damned houseful if you like. Except the jewels. Theyre hired. Will that satisfy you? (*He turns on his heel and is about to go in extreme dudgeon.*)

LIZA (*drinking in his emotion like nectar, and nagging him to provoke a further supply*): Stop, please. (*She takes off her jewels.*) Will you take these to your room and keep them safe? I dont want to run the risk of their being missing.

HIGGINS (*furious*): Hand them over. (*She puts them into his hands.*) If these belonged to me instead of to the jeweller, I'd ram them down your ungrateful throat. (*He perfunctorily thrusts them into his pockets, unconsciously decorating himself with the protruding ends of the chains.*)

LIZA (*taking a ring off*): This ring isnt the jeweller's: it's the one you bought me in Brighton. I dont want it now. (*Higgins dashes the ring violently into the fireplace, and turns on her so threateningly that she crouches over the piano with her hands over her face and exclaims*) Dont you hit me.

HIGGINS: Hit you! You infamous creature, how dare you accuse me of such a thing? It is you who have hit me. You have wounded me to the heart.

LIZA (*thrilling with hidden joy*): I'm glad. Ive got a little of my own back, anyhow.

HIGGINS (*with dignity, in his finest professional style*): You have caused me to lose my temper: a thing that has hardly ever happened to me before. I prefer to say nothing more tonight. I am going to bed.

LIZA (*pertly*): Youd better leave a note for Mrs Pearce about the coffee; for she wont be told by me.

HIGGINS (*formally*): Damn Mrs Pearce; and damn the coffee; and damn you; and (*wildly*) damn my own folly in having lavished my hard-earned knowledge and the treasure of my regard and intimacy on a heartless gutter-snipe. (*He goes out with impressive decorum, and spoils it by slamming the door savagely.*)

(*Eliza goes down on her knees on the hearthrug to look for the ring. When she finds it she considers for a moment what to do with it. Finally she flings it down on the dessert stand and goes upstairs in a tearing rage.*)

*　　*　　*

The furniture of Eliza's room has been increased by a big wardrobe and a sumptuous dressing-table. She comes in and switches on the electric light. She goes to the wardrobe; opens it; and pulls out a walking dress, a hat, and a pair of shoes, which she throws on the bed. She takes off her evening dress and shoes; then takes a padded hanger from the wardrobe; adjusts it carefully in the evening dress; and hangs it in the wardrobe, which she shuts with a slam. She puts on her walking shoes, her walking dress, and hat. She takes her wrist watch from the dressing-table and fastens it on. She pulls on her gloves; takes her vanity bag; and looks into it to see that her purse is there before hanging it on her wrist. She makes for the door. Every movement expresses her furious resolution.

She takes a last look at herself in the glass.

She suddenly puts out her tongue at herself; then leaves the room, switching off the electric light at the door.

Meanwhile, in the street outside, Freddy Eynsford Hill, lovelorn, is gazing up at the second floor, in which one of the windows is still lighted.

The light goes out.

FREDDY: Goodnight, darling, darling, darling.

(*Eliza comes out, giving the door a considerable bang behind her.*)

LIZA: Whatever are you doing here?

FREDDY: Nothing. I spend most of my nights here. It's

the only place where I'm happy. Dont laugh at me, Miss Doolittle.

LIZA: Dont you call me Miss Doolittle, do you hear? Liza's good enough for me. (*She breaks down and grabs him by the shoulders.*) Freddy: you dont think I'm a heartless guttersnipe, do you?

FREDDY: Oh no, no, darling: how can you imagine such a thing? You are the loveliest, dearest—

(*He loses all self-control and smothers her with kisses. She, hungry for comfort, responds. They stand there in one another's arms.*

(*An elderly police constable arrives.*)

CONSTABLE (*scandalized*): Now then! Now then!! Now then!!!

(*They release one another hastily.*)

FREDDY: Sorry, constable. Weve only just become engaged.

(*They run away.*)

The constable shakes his head, reflecting on his own courtship and on the vanity of human hopes. He moves off in the opposite direction with slow professional steps.

The flight of the lovers takes them to Cavendish Square. There they halt to consider their next move.

LIZA (*out of breath*): He didnt half give me a fright, that copper. But you answered him proper.

FREDDY: I hope I havent taken you out of your way. Where were you going?

LIZA: To the river.

FREDDY: What for?

LIZA: To make a hole in it.

FREDDY (*horrified*): Eliza, darling. What do you mean? What's the matter?

LIZA: Never mind. It doesnt matter now. There's nobody in the world now but you and me, is there?

FREDDY: Not a soul.

(*They indulge in another embrace, and are again surprised by a much younger constable.*)

SECOND CONSTABLE: Now then, you two! What's this?

Where do you think you are? Move along here, double quick.

FREDDY: As you say, sir, double quick.

They run away again, and are in Hanover Square before they stop for another conference.

FREDDY: I had no idea the police were so devilishly prudish.

LIZA: It's their business to hunt girls off the streets.

FREDDY: We must go somewhere. We cant wander about the streets all night.

LIZA: Cant we? I think it'd be lovely to wander about for ever.

FREDDY: Oh, darling.

(*They embrace again, oblivious of the arrival of a crawling taxi. It stops.*)

TAXIMAN: Can I drive you and the lady anywhere, sir? (*They start asunder.*)

LIZA: Oh, Freddy, a taxi. The very thing.

FREDDY: But, damn it, I've no money.

LIZA: I have plenty. The Colonel thinks you should never go out without ten pounds in your pocket. Listen. We'll drive about all night; and in the morning I'll call on old Mrs Higgins and ask her what I ought to do. I'll tell you all about it in the cab. And the police wont touch us there.

FREDDY: Righto! Ripping. (*To the Taximan*) Wimbledon Common. (*They drive off.*)

ACT FIVE

Mrs Higgins's drawing room. She is at her writing-table as before. The parlormaid comes in.

THE PARLORMAID (*at the door*): Mr Henry, maam, is downstairs with Colonel Pickering.

MRS HIGGINS: Well, shew them up.

THE PARLORMAID: Theyre using the telephone, maam. Telephoning to the police, I think.

MRS HIGGINS: What!

THE PARLORMAID (*coming further in and lowering her voice*): Mr Henry is in a state, maam. I thought I'd better tell you.

MRS HIGGINS: If you had told me that Mr Henry was not in a state it would have been more surprising. Tell them to come up when theyve finished with the police. I suppose he's lost something.

THE PARLORMAID: Yes, maam (*going*).

MRS HIGGINS: Go upstairs and tell Miss Doolittle that Mr Henry and the Colonel are here. Ask her not to come down til I send for her.

THE PARLORMAID: Yes, maam.

(*Higgins bursts in. He is, as the parlormaid has said, in a state.*)

HIGGINS: Look here, mother: heres a confounded thing!

MRS HIGGINS: Yes, dear. Good morning. (*He checks his impatience and kisses her, whilst the parlormaid goes out.*) What is it?

HIGGINS: Eliza's bolted.

MRS HIGGINS (*calmly continuing her writing*): You must have frightened her.

HIGGINS: Frightened her! nonsense! She was left last night, as usual, to turn out the lights and all that; and instead of going to bed she changed her clothes and went right off: her bed wasnt slept in. She came in a cab for her things before seven this morning; and that fool Mrs Pearce let her have them without telling me a word about it. What am I to do?

MRS HIGGINS: Do without, I'm afraid, Henry. The girl has a perfect right to leave if she chooses.

HIGGINS (*wandering distractedly across the room*): But I cant find anything. I dont know what appointments Ive got. I'm— (*Pickering comes in. Mrs Higgins puts down her pen and turns away from the writing-table.*)

PICKERING (*shaking hands*): Good morning, Mrs Higgins. Has Henry told you? (*He sits down on the ottoman.*)

HIGGINS: What does that ass of an inspector say? Have you offered a reward?

MRS HIGGINS (*rising in indignant amazement*): You dont mean to say you have set the police after Eliza.

HIGGINS: Of course. What are the police for? What else could we do? (*He sits in the Elizabethan chair.*)

PICKERING: The inspector made a lot of difficulties. I really think he suspected us of some improper purpose.

MRS HIGGINS: Well, of course he did. What right have you to go to the police and give the girl's name as if she were a thief, or a lost umbrella, or something? Really! (*She sits down again, deeply vexed.*)

HIGGINS: But we want to find her.

PICKERING: We cant let her go like this, you know, Mrs Higgins. What were we to do?

MRS HIGGINS: You have no more sense, either of you, than two children. Why—

(*The parlormaid comes in and breaks off the conversation.*)

THE PARLORMAID: Mr Henry: a gentleman wants to see

you very particular. He's been sent on from Wimpole Street.

HIGGINS: Oh, bother! I cant see anyone now. Who is it?

THE PARLORMAID: A Mr Doolittle, sir.

PICKERING: Doolittle! Do you mean the dustman?

THE PARLORMAID: Dustman! Oh no, sir: a gentleman.

HIGGINS (*springing up excitedly*): By George, Pick, it's some relative of hers that she's gone to. Somebody we know nothing about. (*To the parlormaid*) Send him up, quick.

THE PARLORMAID: Yes, sir. (*She goes.*)

HIGGINS (*eagerly, going to his mother*): Genteel relatives! now we shall hear something. (*He sits down in the Chippendale chair.*)

MRS HIGGINS: Do you know any of her people?

PICKERING: Only her father: the fellow we told you about.

THE PARLORMAID (*announcing*): Mr Doolittle. (*She withdraws.*)

(*Doolittle enters. He is resplendently dressed as for a fashionable wedding, and might, in fact, be the bridegroom. A flower in his buttonhole, a dazzling silk hat, and patent leather shoes complete the effect. He is too concerned with the business he has come on to notice Mrs Higgins. He walks straight to Higgins, and accosts him with vehement reproach.*)

DOOLITTLE (*indicating his own person*): See here! Do you see this? You done this.

HIGGINS: Done what, man?

DOOLITTLE: This, I tell you. Look at it. Look at this hat. Look at this coat.

PICKERING: Has Eliza been buying you clothes?

DOOLITTLE: Eliza! not she. Why would she buy me clothes?

MRS HIGGINS: Good morning, Mr Doolittle. Wont you sit down?

DOOLITTLE (*taken aback as he becomes conscious that*

he has forgotten his hostess): Asking your pardon, maam. (*He approaches her and shakes her proffered hand.*) Thank you. (*He sits down on the ottoman, on Pickering's right.*) I am that full of what has happened to me that I cant think of anything else.

HIGGINS: What the dickens has happened to you?

DOOLITTLE: I shouldnt mind if it had only happened to me: anything might happen to anybody and nobody to blame but Providence, as you might say. But this is something that you done to me: yes, you, Enry Iggins.

HIGGINS: Have you found Eliza?

DOOLITTLE: Have you lost her?

HIGGINS: Yes.

DOOLITTLE: You have all the luck, you have. I aint found her; but she'll find me quick enough now after what you done to me.

MRS HIGGINS: But what has my son done to you, Mr Doolittle?

DOOLITTLE: Done to me! Ruined me. Destroyed my happiness. Tied me up and delivered me into the hands of middle class morality.

HIGGINS (*rising intolerantly and standing over Doolittle*): Youre raving. Youre drunk. Youre mad. I gave you five pounds. After that I had two conversations with you, at half-a-crown an hour. Ive never seen you since.

DOOLITTLE: Oh! Drunk am I? Mad am I? Tell me this. Did you or did you not write a letter to an old blighter in America that was giving five millions to found Moral Reform Societies all over the world, and that wanted you to invent a univcrsal language for him?

HIGGINS: What! Ezra D. Wannafeller! He's dead. (*He sits down again carelessly.*)

DOOLITTLE: Yes: he's dead; and I'm done for. Now did you or did you not write a letter to him to say that the most original moralist at present in England, to the best of your knowledge, was Alfred Doolittle, a common dustman?

HIGGINS: Oh, after your first visit I remember making some silly joke of the kind.

DOOLITTLE: Ah! you may well call it a silly joke. It
put the lid on me right enough. Just give him the chance
he wanted to shew that Americans is not like us: that
they reckonize and respect merit in every class of life,
however humble. Them words is in his blooming will, in
which, Henry Higgins, thanks to your silly joking, he
leaves me a share in his Predigested Cheese Trust worth
three thousand a year on condition that I lecture for his
Wannafeller Moral Reform World League as often as
they ask me up to six times a year.

HIGGINS: The devil he does! Whew! (*Brightening suddenly*) What a lark!

PICKERING: A safe thing for you, Doolittle. They wont
ask you twice.

DOOLITTLE: It aint the lecturing I mind. I'll lecture
them blue in the face, I will, and not turn a hair. It's
making a gentleman of me that I object to. Who asked
him to make a gentleman of me? I was happy. I was
free. I touched pretty nigh everybody for money when
I wanted it, same as I touched you, Enry Iggins. Now I
am worrited; tied neck and heels; and everybody touches
me for money. It's a fine thing for you, says my solicitor.
Is it? says I. You mean it's a good thing for you, I says.
When I was a poor man and had a solicitor once when
they found a pram in the dust cart, he got me off, and
got shut of me and got me shut of him as quick as he
could. Same with the doctors: used to shove me out of
the hospital before I could hardly stand on my legs, and
nothing to pay. Now they finds out that I'm not a healthy
man and cant live unless they looks after me twice a
day. In the house I'm not let do a hand's turn for myself:
somebody else must do it and touch me for it. A year
ago I hadnt a relative in the world except two or three
that wouldnt speak to me. Now Ive fifty, and not a
decent week's wages among the lot of them. I have to
live for others and not for myself: thats middle class
morality. You talk of losing Eliza. Dont you be anxious:
I bet she's on my doorstep by this: she that could support herself easy by selling flowers if I wasnt respectable.

And the next one to touch me will be you, Enry Iggins. I'll have to learn to speak middle class language from you, instead of speaking proper English. Thats where youll come in; and I daresay thats what you done it for.

MRS HIGGINS: But, my dear Mr Doolittle, you need not suffer all this if you are really in earnest. Nobody can force you to accept this bequest. You can repudiate it. Isnt that so, Colonel Pickering?

PICKERING: I believe so.

DOOLITTLE (*softening his manner in deference to her sex*): Thats the tragedy of it, maam. It's easy to say chuck it; but I havnt the nerve. Which of us has? We're all intimidated. Intimidated, maam: thats what we are. What is there for me if I chuck it but the workhouse in my old age? I have to dye my hair already to keep my job as a dustman. If I was one of the deserving poor, and had put by a bit, I could chuck it; but then why should I, acause the deserving poor might as well be millionaires for all the happiness they ever has. They dont know what happiness is. But I, as one of the undeserving poor, have nothing between me and the pauper's uniform but this here blasted three thousand a year that shoves me into the middle class. (Excuse the expression, maam; youd use it yourself if you had my provocation.) Theyve got you every way you turn: it's a choice between the Skilly of the workhouse and the Char Bydis of the middle class; and I havnt the nerve for the workhouse. Intimidated: thats what I am. Broke. Bought up. Happier men than me will call for my dust, and touch me for their tip; and I'll look on helpless, and cnvy them. And thats what your son has brought me to. (*He is overcome by emotion.*)

MRS HIGGINS: Well, I'm very glad youre not going to do anything foolish, Mr Doolittle. For this solves the problem of Eliza's future. You can provide for her now.

DOOLITTLE (*with melancholy resignation*): Yes, maam: I'm expected to provide for everyone now, out of three thousand a year.

HIGGINS (*jumping up*): Nonsense! he cant provide for her. He shant provide for her. She doesnt belong to him.

I paid him five pounds for her. Doolittle: either youre an honest man or a rogue.

DOOLITTLE (*tolerantly*): A little of both, Henry, like the rest of us: a little of both.

HIGGINS: Well, you took that money for the girl; and you have no right to take her as well.

MRS HIGGINS: Henry: dont be absurd. If you want to know where Eliza is, she is upstairs.

HIGGINS (*amazed*): Upstairs!!! Then I shall jolly soon fetch her downstairs. (*He makes resolutely for the door.*)

MRS HIGGINS (*rising and following him*): Be quiet, Henry. Sit down.

HIGGINS: I—

MRS HIGGINS: Sit down, dear; and listen to me.

HIGGINS: Oh very well, very well, very well. (*He throws himself ungraciously on the ottoman, with his face towards the windows.*) But I think you might have told us this half an hour ago.

MRS HIGGINS: Eliza came to me this morning. She told me of the brutal way you two treated her.

HIGGINS (*bounding up again*): What!

PICKERING (*rising also*): My dear Mrs Higgins, she's been telling you stories. We didnt treat her brutally. We hardly said a word to her; and we parted on particularly good terms. (*Turning on Higgins*) Higgins: did you bully her after I went to bed?

HIGGINS: Just the other way about. She threw my slippers in my face. She behaved in the most outrageous way. I never gave her the slightest provocation. The slippers came bang into my face the moment I entered the room—before I had uttered a word. And used perfectly awful language.

PICKERING (*astonished*): But why? What did we do to her?

MRS HIGGINS: I think I know pretty well what you did. The girl is naturally rather affectionate, I think. Isnt she, Mr Doolittle?

DOOLITTLE: Very tender-hearted, maam. Takes after me.

MRS HIGGINS: Just so. She had become attached to you both. She worked very hard for you, Henry. I dont think you quite realize what anything in the nature of brain work means to a girl of her class. Well, it seems that when the great day of trial came, and she did this wonderful thing for you without making a single mistake, you two sat there and never said a word to her, but talked together of how glad you were that it was all over and how you had been bored with the whole thing. And then you were surprised because she threw your slippers at you! *I* should have thrown the fire-irons at you.

HIGGINS: We said nothing except that we were tired and wanted to go to bed. Did we, Pick?

PICKERING (*shrugging his shoulders*): That was all.

MRS HIGGINS (*ironically*): Quite sure?

PICKERING: Absolutely. Really, that was all.

MRS HIGGINS: You didnt thank her, or pet her, or admire her, or tell her how splendid she'd been.

HIGGINS (*impatiently*): But she knew all about that. We didnt make speeches to her, if thats what you mean.

PICKERING (*conscience stricken*): Perhaps we were a little inconsiderate. Is she very angry?

MRS HIGGINS (*returning to her place at the writing-table*): Well, I'm afraid she wont go back to Wimpole Street, especially now that Mr Doolittle is able to keep up the position you have thrust on her; but she says she is quite willing to meet you on friendly terms and to let bygones be bygones.

HIGGINS (*furious*): Is she, by George? Ho!

MRS HIGGINS: If you promise to behave yourself, Henry, I'll ask her to come down. If not, go home; for you have taken up quite enough of my time.

HIGGINS: Oh, all right. Very well. Pick: you behave yourself. Let us put on our best Sunday manners for this creature that we picked out of the mud. (*He flings himself sulkily into the Elizabethan chair.*)

DOOLITTLE (*remonstrating*): Now, now, Enry Iggins! Have some consideration for my feelings as a middle class man.

MRS HIGGINS: Remember your promise, Henry. (*She presses the bell-button on the writing-table.*) Mr Doolittle: will you be so good as to step out on the balcony for a moment. I dont want Eliza to have the shock of your news until she has made it up with these two gentlemen. Would you mind?

DOOLITTLE: As you wish, lady. Anything to help Henry to keep her off my hands. (*He disappears through the window.*)

(*The parlormaid answers the bell. Pickering sits down in Doolittle's place.*)

MRS HIGGINS: Ask Miss Doolittle to come down, please.

THE PARLORMAID: Yes, maam. (*She goes out.*)

MRS HIGGINS: Now, Henry: be good.

HIGGINS: I am behaving myself perfectly.

PICKERING: He is doing his best, Mrs Higgins.

(*A pause. Higgins throws back his head; stretches out his legs; and begins to whistle.*)

MRS HIGGINS: Henry, dearest, you dont look at all nice in that attitude.

HIGGINS (*pulling himself together*): I was not trying to look nice, mother.

MRS HIGGINS: It doesnt matter, dear. I only wanted to make you speak.

HIGGINS: Why?

MRS HIGGINS: Because you cant speak and whistle at the same time.

(*Higgins groans. Another very trying pause.*)

HIGGINS (*springing up, out of patience*): Where the devil is that girl? Are we to wait here all day?

(*Eliza enters, sunny, self-possessed, and giving a staggeringly convincing exhibition of ease of manner. She carries a little work-basket, and is very much at home. Pickering is too much taken aback to rise.*)

LIZA: How do you do, Professor Higgins? Are you quite well?

HIGGINS (*choking*): Am I— (*He can say no more.*)

LIZA: But of course you are: you are never ill. So glad

to see you again, Colonel Pickering. (*He rises hastily; and they shake hands.*) Quite chilly this morning, isnt it? (*She sits down on his left. He sits beside her.*)

HIGGINS: Dont you dare try this game on me. I taught it to you; and it doesnt take me in. Get up and come home; and dont be a fool.

(*Eliza takes a piece of needlework from her basket, and begins to stitch at it, without taking the least notice of this outburst.*)

MRS HIGGINS: Very nicely put, indeed, Henry. No woman could resist such an invitation.

HIGGINS: You let her alone, mother. Let her speak for herself. You will jolly soon see whether she has an idea that I havnt put into her head or a word that I havnt put into her mouth. I tell you I have created this thing out of the squashed cabbage leaves of Covent Garden; and now she pretends to play the fine lady with me.

MRS HIGGINS (*placidly*): Yes, dear; but youll sit down, wont you?

(*Higgins sits down again, savagely.*)

LIZA (*to Pickering, taking no apparent notice of Higgins, and working away deftly*): Will you drop me altogether now that the experiment is over, Colonel Pickering?

PICKERING: Oh dont. You mustnt think of it as an experiment. It shocks me, somehow.

LIZA: Oh, I'm only a squashed cabbage leaf—

PICKERING (*impulsively*): No.

LIZA (*continuing quietly*) —but I owe so much to you that I should be very unhappy if you forgot me.

PICKERING: It's very kind of you to say so, Miss Doolittle.

LIZA: It's not because you paid for my dresses. I know you are generous to everybody with money. But it was from you that I learnt really nice manners, and that is what makes one a lady, isnt it? You see it was so very difficult for me with the example of Professor Higgins always before me. I was brought up to be just like him, unable to control myself, and using bad language on the slightest provocation. And I should never have known that ladies and gentlemen didnt behave like that if you hadnt been there.

HIGGINS: Well!!

PICKERING: Oh, thats only his way, you know. He doesnt mean it.

LIZA: Oh, *I* didnt mean it either, when I was a flower girl. It was only my way. But you see I did it; and thats what makes the difference after all.

PICKERING: No doubt. Still, he taught you to speak; and I couldnt have done that, you know.

LIZA (*trivially*): Of course: that is his profession.

HIGGINS: Damnation!

LIZA (*continuing*): It was just like learning to dance in the fashionable way: there was nothing more than that in it. But do you know what began my real education?

PICKERING: What?

LIZA (*stopping her work for a moment*): Your calling me Miss Doolittle that day when I first came to Wimpole Street. That was the beginning of self-respect for me. (*She resumes her stitching.*) And there were a hundred little things you never noticed, because they came naturally to you. Things about standing up and taking off your hat and opening doors—

PICKERING: Oh, that was nothing.

LIZA: Yes: things that shewed you thought and felt about me as if I were something better than a scullery-maid; though of course I know you would have been just the same to a scullery-maid if she had been let into the drawing room. You never took off your boots in the dining room when I was there.

PICKERING: You mustnt mind that. Higgins takes off his boots all over the place.

LIZA: I know. I am not blaming him. It is his way, isnt it? But it made such a difference to me that you didnt do it. You see, really and truly, apart from the things anyone can pick up (the dressing and the proper way of speaking, and so on), the difference between a lady and a flower girl is not how she behaves, but how she's treated. I shall always be a flower girl to Professor Higgins, because he always treats me as a flower girl, and always will; but I know I can be a lady to you, because you always treat me as a lady, and always will.

MRS HIGGINS: Please dont grind your teeth, Henry.

PICKERING: Well, this is really very nice of you, Miss Doolittle.

LIZA: I should like you to call me Eliza, now, if you would.

PICKERING: Thank you. Eliza, of course.

LIZA: And I should like Professor Higgins to call me Miss Doolittle.

HIGGINS: I'll see you damned first.

MRS HIGGINS: Henry! Henry!

PICKERING (*laughing*): Why dont you slang back at him? Dont stand it. It would do him a lot of good.

LIZA: I cant. I could have done it once; but now I cant go back to it. You told me, you know, that when a child is brought to a foreign country, it picks up the language in a few weeks, and forgets its own. Well, I am a child in your country. I have forgotten my own language, and can speak nothing but yours. Thats the real break-off with the corner of Tottenham Court Road. Leaving Wimpole Street finishes it.

PICKERING (*much alarmed*): Oh! but youre coming back to Wimpole Street, arnt you? Youll forgive Higgins?

HIGGINS (*rising*): Forgive! Will she, by George! Let her go. Let her find out how she can get on without us. She will relapse into the gutter in three weeks without me at her elbow.

(*Doolittle appears at the centre window. With a look of dignified reproach at Higgins, he comes slowly and silently to his daughter, who, with her back to the window, is unconscious of his approach.*)

PICKERING: He's incorrigible, Eliza. You wont relapse, will you?

LIZA: No: not now. Never again. I have learnt my lesson. I dont believe I could utter one of the old sounds if I tried. (*Doolittle touches her on her left shoulder. She drops her work, losing her self-possession utterly at the spectacle of her father's splendor.*) A-a-a-a-a-ah-ow-ooh!

HIGGINS (*with a crow of triumph*): Aha! Just so. A-a-a-a-ahowooh! A-a-a-a-ahowooh! A-a-a-a-ahowooh! Victory! Victory! (*He throws himself on the divan, folding his arms, and spraddling arrogantly.*)

DOOLITTLE: Can you blame the girl? Dont look at me like that, Eliza. It aint my fault. Ive come into some money.

LIZA: You must have touched a millionaire this time, dad.

DOOLITTLE: I have. But I'm dressed something special today. I'm going to St George's, Hanover Square. Your stepmother is going to marry me.

LIZA (*angrily*): Youre going to let yourself down to marry that low common woman!

PICKERING (*quietly*): He ought to, Eliza. (*To Doolittle*) Why has she changed her mind?

DOOLITTLE (*sadly*): Intimidated, Governor. Intimidated. Middle class morality claims its victim. Wont you put on your hat, Liza, and come and see me turned off?

LIZA: If the Colonel says I must, I—I'll (*almost sobbing*) I'll demean myself. And get insulted for my pains, like enough.

DOOLITTLE: Dont be afraid: she never comes to words with anyone now, poor woman! respectability has broke all the spirit out of her.

PICKERING (*squeezing Eliza's elbow gently*): Be kind to them, Eliza. Make the best of it.

LIZA (*forcing a little smile for him through her vexation*): Oh well, just to shew theres no ill feeling. I'll be back in a moment. (*She goes out.*)

DOOLITTLE (*sitting down beside Pickering*): I feel uncommon nervous about the ceremony, Colonel. I wish youd come and see me through it.

PICKERING: But youve been through it before, man. You were married to Eliza's mother.

DOOLITTLE: Who told you that, Colonel?

PICKERING: Well, nobody told me. But I concluded—naturally—

DOOLITTLE: No: that aint the natural way, Colonel; it's only the middle class way. My way was always the undeserving way. But dont say nothing to Eliza. She dont know: I always had a delicacy about telling her.

PICKERING: Quite right. We'll leave it so, if you dont mind.

DOOLITTLE: And youll come to the church, Colonel, and put me through straight?

PICKERING: With pleasure. As far as a bachelor can.

MRS HIGGINS: May I come, Mr Doolittle? I should be very sorry to miss your wedding.

DOOLITTLE: I should indeed be honored by your condescension, maam; and my poor old woman would take it as a tremenjous compliment. She's been very low, thinking of the happy days that are no more.

MRS HIGGINS (*rising*): I'll order the carriage and get ready. (*The men rise, except Higgins.*) I shant be more than fifteen minutes. (*As she goes to the door Eliza comes in, hatted and buttoning her gloves.*) I'm going to the church to see your father married, Eliza. You had better come in the brougham with me. Colonel Pickering can go on with the bridegroom.

(*Mrs Higgins goes out. Eliza comes to the middle of the room between the centre window and the ottoman. Pickering joins her.*)

DOOLITTLE: Bridegroom! What a word! It makes a man realize his position, somchow. (*He takes up his hat and goes towards the door.*)

PICKERING: Before I go, Eliza, do forgive Higgins and come back to us.

LIZA: I dont think dad would allow me. Would you, dad?

DOOLITTLE (*sad but magnanimous*): They played you off very cunning, Eliza, them two sportsmen. If it had been only one of them, you could have nailed him. But you see, there was two; and one of them chaperoned the other, as you might say. (*To Pickering*) It was artful of you, Colonel; but I bear no malice: I should have done the same myself. I been the victim of one woman after another all my life; and I dont grudge you two getting the better of Eliza. I shant interfere. It's time for us to go, Colonel. So long, Henry. See you in St George's, Eliza. (*He goes out.*)

PICKERING (*coaxing*): Do stay with us, Eliza. (*He follows Doolittle.*)

(*Eliza goes out on the balcony to avoid being alone with Higgins. He rises and joins her there. She immediately comes back into the room and makes for the door; but he goes along the balcony quickly and gets his back to the door before she reaches it.*)

HIGGINS: Well, Eliza, youve had a bit of your own back, as you call it. Have you had enough? and are you going to be reasonable? Or do you want any more?

LIZA: You want me back only to pick up your slippers and put up with your tempers and fetch and carry for you.

HIGGINS: I havnt said I wanted you back at all.

LIZA: Oh, indeed. Then what are we talking about?

HIGGINS: About you, not about me. If you come back I shall treat you just as I have always treated you. I cant change my nature; and I dont intend to change my manners. My manners are exactly the same as Colonel Pickering's.

LIZA: Thats not true. He treats a flower girl as if she was a duchess.

HIGGINS: And I treat a duchess as if she was a flower girl.

LIZA: I see. (*She turns away composedly, and sits on the ottoman, facing the window.*) The same to everybody.

HIGGINS: Just so.

LIZA: Like father.

HIGGINS (*grinning, a little taken down*): Without accepting the comparison at all points, Eliza, it's quite true that your father is not a snob, and that he will be quite at home in any station of life to which his eccentric destiny may call him. (*Seriously*) The great secret, Eliza, is not having bad manners or good manners or any other

particular sort of manners, but having the same manners
for all human souls: in short, behaving as if you were in
Heaven, where there are no third-class carriages, and
one soul is as good as another.

LIZA: Amen. You are a born preacher.

HIGGINS (*irritated*): The question is not whether I treat
you rudely, but whether you ever heard me treat anyone
else better.

LIZA (*with sudden sincerity*): I dont care how you treat
me. I dont mind your swearing at me. I shouldnt mind
a black eye: Ive had one before this. But (*standing up
and facing him*) I wont be passed over.

HIGGINS: Then get out of my way; for I wont stop for
you. You talk about me as if I were a motor bus.

LIZA: So you are a motor bus: all bounce and go, and
no consideration for anyone. But I can do without you:
dont think I cant.

HIGGINS: I know you can. I told you you could.

LIZA (*wounded, getting away from him to the other
side of the ottoman with her face to the hearth*): I know
you did, you brute. You wanted to get rid of me.

HIGGINS: Liar.

LIZA: Thank you. (*She sits down with dignity.*)

HIGGINS: You never asked yourself, I suppose, whether
I could do without you.

LIZA (*earnestly*): Dont you try to get round me. Youll
have to do without me.

HIGGINS (*arrogant*): I can do without anybody. I have
my own soul: my own spark of divine fire. But (*with
sudden humility*) I shall miss you, Eliza. (*He sits down
near her on the ottoman.*) I have learnt something from
your idiotic notions: I confess that humbly and gratefully. And I have grown accustomed to your voice and
appearance. I like them, rather.

LIZA: Well, you have both of them on your gramophone and in your book of photographs. When you feel
lonely without me, you can turn the machine on. It's got
no feelings to hurt.

HIGGINS: I cant turn your soul on. Leave me those

feelings; and you can take away the voice and the face. They are not you.

LIZA: Oh, you are a devil. You can twist the heart in a girl as easy as some could twist her arms to hurt her. Mrs Pearce warned me. Time and again she has wanted to leave you; and you always got round her at the last minute. And you dont care a bit for her. And you dont care a bit for me.

HIGGINS: I care for life, for humanity; and you are a part of it that has come my way and been built into my house. What more can you or anyone ask?

LIZA: I wont care for anybody that doesnt care for me.

HIGGINS: Commercial principles, Eliza. Like (*reproducing her Covent Garden pronunciation with professional exactness*) s'yollin voylets [selling violets], isnt it?

LIZA: Dont sneer at me. It's mean to sneer at me.

HIGGINS: I have never sneered in my life. Sneering doesnt become either the human face or the human soul. I am expressing my righteous contempt for Commercialism. I dont and wont trade in affection. You call me a brute because you couldnt buy a claim on me by fetching my slippers and finding my spectacles. You were a fool: I think a woman fetching a man's slippers is a disgusting sight: did I ever fetch your slippers? I think a good deal more of you for throwing them in my face. No use slaving for me and then saying you want to be cared for: who cares for a slave? If you come back, come back for the sake of good fellowship; for youll get nothing else. Youve had a thousand times as much out of me as I have out of you; and if you dare to set up your little dog's tricks of fetching and carrying slippers against my creation of a Duchess Eliza, I'll slam the door in your silly face.

LIZA: What did you do it for if you didnt care for me?

HIGGINS (*heartily*): Why, because it was my job.

LIZA: You never thought of the trouble it would make for me.

HIGGINS: Would the world ever have been made if its maker had been afraid of making trouble? Making life means making trouble. Theres only one way of escaping trouble; and thats killing things. Cowards, you notice, are always shrieking to have troublesome people killed.

LIZA: I'm no preacher: I dont notice things like that. I notice that you dont notice me.

HIGGINS (*jumping up and walking about intolerantly*): Eliza: youre an idiot. I waste the treasures of my Miltonic mind by spreading them before you. Once for all, understand that I go my way and do my work without caring twopence what happens to either of us. I am not intimidated, like your father and your stepmother. So you can come back or go to the devil: which you please.

LIZA: What am I to come back for?

HIGGINS (*bouncing up on his knees on the ottoman and leaning over it to her*): For the fun of it. Thats why I took you on.

LIZA (*with averted face*): And you may throw me out tomorrow if I dont do everything you want me to?

HIGGINS: Yes; and you may walk out tomorrow if I dont do everything you want me to.

LIZA: And live with my stepmother?

HIGGINS: Yes, or sell flowers.

LIZA: Oh! if I only could go back to my flower basket! I should be independent of both you and father and all the world! Why did you take my independence from me? Why did I give it up? I'm a slave now, for all my fine clothes.

HIGGINS: Not a bit. I'll adopt you as my daughter and settle money on you if you like. Or would you rather marry Pickering?

LIZA (*looking fiercely round at him*): I wouldnt marry you if you asked me; and youre nearer my age than what he is.

HIGGINS (*gently*): Than he is: not "than what he is."

LIZA (*losing her temper and rising*): I'll talk as I like. Youre not my teacher now.

HIGGINS (*reflectively*): I dont suppose Pickering would, though. He's as confirmed an old bachelor as I am.

LIZA: Thats not what I want; and dont you think it.

Ive always had chaps enough wanting me that way. Freddy Hill writes to me twice and three times a day, sheets and sheets.

HIGGINS (*disagreeably surprised*): Damn his impudence! (*He recoils and finds himself sitting on his heels.*)

LIZA: He has a right to if he likes, poor lad. And he does love me.

HIGGINS (*getting off the ottoman*): You have no right to encourage him.

LIZA: Every girl has a right to be loved.

HIGGINS: What! By fools like that?

LIZA: Freddy's not a fool. And if he's weak and poor and wants me, may be he'd make me happier than my betters that bully me and dont want me.

HIGGINS: Can he make anything of you? Thats the point.

LIZA: Perhaps I could make something of him. But I never thought of us making anything of one another; and you never think of anything else. I only want to be natural.

HIGGINS: In short, you want me to be as infatuated about you as Freddy? Is that it?

LIZA: No I dont. That's not the sort of feeling I want from you. And dont you be too sure of yourself or of me. I could have been a bad girl if I'd liked. Ive seen more of some things than you, for all your learning. Girls like me can drag gentlemen down to make love to them easy enough. And they wish each other dead the next minute.

HIGGINS: Of course they do. Then what in thunder are we quarrelling about?

LIZA (*much troubled*): I want a little kindness. I know I'm a common ignorant girl, and you a book-learned gentleman; but I'm not dirt under your feet. What I done (*correcting herself*) what I did was not for the dresses and the taxis: I did it because we were pleasant together and I come—came—to care for you; not to want you to make love to me, and not forgetting the difference between us, but more friendly like.

HIGGINS: Well, of course. Thats just how I feel. And how Pickering feels. Eliza: youre a fool.

LIZA: Thats not a proper answer to give me. (*She sinks on the chair at the writing-table in tears.*)

HIGGINS: It's all youll get until you stop being a common idiot. If youre going to be a lady, youll have to give up feeling neglected if the men you know dont spend half their time snivelling over you and the other half giving you black eyes. If you cant stand the coldness of my sort of life, and the strain of it, go back to the gutter. Work til youre more a brute than a human being; and then cuddle and squabble and drink til you fall asleep. Oh, it's a fine life, the life of the gutter. It's real: it's warm: it's violent: you can feel it through the thickest skin: you can taste it and smell it without any training or any work. Not like Science and Literature and Classical Music and Philosophy and Art. You find me cold, unfeeling, selfish, dont you? Very well: be off with you to the sort of people you like. Marry some sentimental hog or other with lots of money, and a thick pair of lips to kiss you with and a thick pair of boots to kick you with. If you cant appreciate what youve got, youd better get what you can appreciate.

LIZA (*desperate*): Oh, you are a cruel tyrant. I cant talk to you: you turn everything against me: I'm always in the wrong. But you know very well all the time that youre nothing but a bully. You know I cant go back to the gutter, as you call it, and that I have no real friends in the world but you and the Colonel. You know well I couldnt bear to live with a low common man after you two; and it's wicked and cruel of you to insult me by pretending I could. You think I must go back to Wimpole Street because I have nowhere else to go but father's. But dont you be too sure that you have me under your feet to be trampled on and talked down. I'll marry Freddy, I will, as soon as I'm able to support him.

HIGGINS (*thunderstruck*): Freddy!!! that young fool! That poor devil who couldnt get a job as an errand boy even if he had the guts to try for it! Woman: do you not understand that I have made you a consort for a king?

LIZA: Freddy loves me: that makes him king enough for me. I dont want him to work: he wasnt brought up to it as I was. I'll go and be a teacher.

HIGGINS: Whatll you teach, in heaven's name?

LIZA: What you taught me. I'll teach phonetics.

HIGGINS: Ha! ha! ha!

LIZA: I'll offer myself as an assistant to that hairy-faced Hungarian.

HIGGINS (*rising in a fury*): What! That impostor! that humbug! that toadying ignoramus! Teach him my methods! my discoveries! You take one step in his direction and I'll wring your neck. (*He lays hands on her.*) Do you hear?

LIZA (*defiantly non-resistant*): Wring away. What do I care? I knew youd strike me some day. (*He lets her go, stamping with rage at having forgotten himself, and recoils so hastily that he stumbles back into his seat on the ottoman.*) Aha! Now I know how to deal with you. What a fool I was not to think of it before! You cant take away the knowledge you gave me. You said I had a finer ear than you. And I can be civil and kind to people, which is more than you can. Aha! (*Purposely dropping her aitches to annoy him*) Thats done you, Enry Iggins, it az. Now I dont care that (*snapping her fingers*) for your bullying and your big talk. I'll advertize it in the papers that your duchess is only a flower girl that you taught, and that she'll teach anybody to be a duchess just the same in six months for a thousand guineas. Oh, when I think of myself crawling under your feet and being trampled on and called names, when all the time I had only to lift up my finger to be as good as you, I could just kick myself.

HIGGINS (*wondering at her*): You damned impudent slut, you! But it's better than snivelling; better than fetching slippers and finding spectacles, isnt it? (*Rising*) By George, Eliza, I said I'd make a woman of you; and I have. I like you like this.

LIZA: Yes: you turn round and make up to me now that I'm not afraid of you, and can do without you.

HIGGINS: Of course I do, you little fool. Five minutes ago you were like a millstone round my neck. Now youre a tower of strength: a consort battleship. You and I and Pickering will be three old bachelors together instead of only two men and a silly girl.

(*Mrs Higgins returns, dressed for the wedding. Eliza instantly becomes cool and elegant.*)

MRS HIGGINS: The carriage is waiting, Eliza. Are you ready?

LIZA: Quite. Is the Professor coming?

MRS HIGGINS: Certainly not. He cant behave himself in church. He makes remarks out loud all the time on the clergyman's pronunciation.

LIZA: Then I shall not see you again, Professor. Goodbye. (*She goes to the door.*)

MRS HIGGINS (*coming to Higgins*): Goodbye, dear.

HIGGINS: Goodbye, mother. (*He is about to kiss her, when he recollects something.*) Oh, by the way, Eliza, order a ham and a Stilton cheese, will you? And buy me a pair of reindeer gloves, number eights, and a tie to match that new suit of mine. You can choose the color. (*His cheerful, careless, vigorous voice shews that he is incorrigible.*)

LIZA (*disdainfully*): Number eights are too small for you if you want them lined with lamb's wool. You have three new ties that you have forgotten in the drawer of your washstand. Colonel Pickering prefers double Gloucester to Stilton; and you dont notice the difference. I telephoned Mrs Pearce this morning not to forget the ham. What you are to do without me I cannot imagine. (*She sweeps out.*)

MRS HIGGINS: I'm afraid youve spoilt that girl, Henry. I should be uneasy about you and her if she were less fond of Colonel Pickering.

HIGGINS: Pickering! Nonsense: she's going to marry Freddy. Ha ha! Freddy! Freddy!! Ha ha ha ha ha!!!!! (*He roars with laughter as the play ends.*)

Shorthand Fragment, 1914

(Possibly intended to be part of a drafted interview. British Museum Add. MSS. 50560, f. 181)

Is Pygmalion irresistibly funny?

Not at all. There is nothing in it to force on anyone the alternative of their being uproarious or bursting. I can listen to it without yells of merriment; and I, as the author, ought to be more amused by it than anyone else. It is really a serious play, although it is the romance of a flower girl changed into a lady by a gentleman whom she meets by accident on a wet night when they are both sheltering from the rain under the portico of St Paul's Church in Covent Garden. But there is a serious side to the play in the fate of the girl's father, whose story is really a modern version of the old Don Juan play "Il dissoluto punito." This man is an Immoralist, a lover of wine, women, and song, a flouter of respectability, one whose delight it is to épater le bourgeois. In the old play he is cast into hell by the statue of the man he has murdered. In my play a far more real and terrible fate overtakes him. No: it is not the fate of Oswald in Ibsen's *Ghosts*, nor of the young man in Brieux's *Les Avariés*. Nothing like that at all. Something quite simple, quite respectable, quite presentable to the youngest schoolgirl. And yet a frightful retribution. The rest of the play is merely to call public attention to the importance of the study of phonetics, which has always been one of my favorite subjects. Let me tell you one remarkable fact. The translation of the play into Swedish by Mr Hugo Vallentin has been made extremely difficult by the fact, astounding to a Londoner, that in Stockholm all classes speak the same language. That is real civilization. Here the flower girl speaks one language and the duchess another; though the difference is not so great as the duchess thinks, especially if she is a smart duchess. We shall never have a standard English until we have a National Theatre co-operating with a serious Academy of Letters. Not that they will do anything, but people will keep saying that they ought to do something; and that is how things finally get done.

All this sounds very serious.

[End of fragment]

Bernard Shaw Flays Filmdom's "Illiterates"

(Replies to a questionnaire by Dennison Thornton, Reynolds News, *London, 22 January 1939)*

If we are to believe what the film producers are always telling us about the low intelligence of the average filmgoer, how do you account for the tremendous success everywhere of "Pygmalion," which has been praised as one of the most intelligent films yet made?

Only thoughtless people chatter about the low intelligence of the average filmgoer. There is no such person. There are several classes of public entertainment, including several classes of film. And there are several classes of film director, including some who are so illiterate that they cannot conceive anyone being interested in anything but very crudely presented police and divorce court news, and adventures out of boys' journals.

They are usually ranked as infallible authorities on the suitability of scenarios. These gentlemen have never had any use for me and I cannot pretend that I have any use for them.

Do you think that these filmed versions of your plays will bring about a new type of film—films in which problems

*of conduct and character of importance to the audience
are raised and suggestively discussed?*

I don't think "Pygmalion" will bring about anything but
the confusion of the idiots who maintain that a good play
must make a bad film, and that the musical English of a
dramatic poet must be converted into the slang of a Californian bar-tender or it will not be understood in Seattle—
where, by the way, they do not speak Californian.

*In a note to the stage version of "Pygmalion," you de-
plored what you called "ready-made, happy endings to
misfit all stories." Yet you allowed such a ready-made
happy ending to be substituted in the film version of
"Pygmalion." Why?*

I did not. I cannot conceive a less happy ending to
the story of "Pygmalion" than a love affair between the
middle-aged, middle-class professor, a confirmed old
bachelor with a mother-fixation, and a flower girl of 18.
Nothing of the kind was emphasised in my scenario,
where I emphasised the escape of Eliza from the tyranny
of Higgins by a quite natural love affair with Freddy.

But I cannot at my age undertake studio work: and
about 20 directors seem to have turned up there and
spent their time trying to sidetrack me and Mr Gabriel
Pascal, who does really know chalk from cheese. They
devised a scene to give a lovelorn complexion at the end
to Mr Leslie Howard: but it is too inconclusive to be
worth making a fuss about.

My Fair Lady

A Musical Play
in Two Acts

Based on Shaw's *Pygmalion*
Adaptation and Lyrics by Alan Jay Lerner
Music by Frederick Loewe

Note

For the published version of *Pygmalion*,* Shaw wrote a preface and an epilogue which he called a sequel. I have omitted the preface because the information contained therein is less pertinent to *My Fair Lady* than it is to *Pygmalion*.

I have omitted the sequel because in it Shaw explains how Eliza ends not with Higgins but with Freddy and—Shaw and Heaven forgive me!—I am not certain he is right.

A.J.L.

[*The Bodley Head Collected Plays, Vol. 4, London.—Ed.]

My Fair Lady

My Fair Lady opened in New York March 15, 1956, at the Mark Hellinger Theatre with the following cast:

(*In order of appearance*)

BUSKERS, *Imelda de Martin, Carl Jeffrey, Joe Rocco*
MRS. EYNSFORD-HILL, *Viola Roache*
ELIZA DOOLITTLE, *Julie Andrews*
FREDDY EYNSFORD-HILL, *Michael King*
COLONEL PICKERING, *Robert Coote*
A BYSTANDER, *Christopher Hewett*
HENRY HIGGINS, *Rex Harrison*
SELSEY MAN, *Gordon Dilworth*
HOXTON MAN, *David Thomas*
ANOTHER BYSTANDER, *Rod McLennan*
FIRST COCKNEY, *Reid Shelton*
SECOND COCKNEY, *Glenn Kezer*
THIRD COCKNEY, *James Morris*
FOURTH COCKNEY, *Herb Surface*
BARTENDER, *David Thomas*
HARRY, *Gordon Dilworth*
JAMIE, *Rod McLennan*
ALFRED P. DOOLITTLE, *Stanley Holloway*
MRS. PEARCE, *Philippa Bevans*
MRS. HOPKINS, *Olive Reeves-Smith*
BUTLER, *Reid Shelton*
SERVANTS, *Rosemary Gaines, Colleen O'Connor, Muriel Shaw, Gloria van Dorpe, Glenn Kezer*
MRS. HIGGINS, *Cathleen Nesbitt*

113

CHAUFFEUR, *Barton Mumaw*

FOOTMEN, *Gordon Ewing, William Krach*

LORD BOXINGTON, *Gordon Dilworth*

LADY BOXINGTON, *Olive Reeves-Smith*

CONSTABLE, *Barton Mumaw*

FLOWER GIRL, *Cathy Conklin*

ZOLTAN KARPATHY, *Christopher Hewett*

FLUNKEY, *Paul Brown*

QUEEN OF TRANSYLVANIA, *Maribel Hammer*

AMBASSADOR, *Rod McLennan*

BARTENDER, *Paul Brown*

MRS. HIGGINS' MAID, *Judith Williams*

SINGING ENSEMBLE, *Melisande Congdon, Lola Fisher, Rosemary Gaines, Maribel Hammer, Colleen O'Connor, Muriel Shaw, Patti Spangler, Gloria van Dorpe, Paul Brown, Gordon Ewing, Glenn Kezer, William Krach, James Morris, Reid Shelton, Herb Surface, David Thomas*

DANCING ENSEMBLE, *Estelle Aza, Cathy Conklin, Margaret Cuddy, Imelda de Martin, Pat Diamond, Pat Drylie, Barbara Heath, Vera Lee, Nancy Lynch, Judith Williams, Thatcher Clarke, Crandall Diehl, David Evans, Carl Jeffrey, Barton Mumaw, Gene Nettles, Paul Olson, Joe Rocco, Fernando Schaffenburg, James White*

My Fair Lady was produced by Herman Levin
Directed by Moss Hart
Scenery by Oliver Smith
Costumes by Cecil Beaton
Choreography by Hanya Holm
Lighting by Feder
Orchestra conducted by Franz Allers
Orchestration by Robert Russell Bennet and Phil Lang

Musical Synopsis

Act One

1. Street Entertainers	THE 3 BUSKERS
2. "Why Can't the English?"	HIGGINS
3. "Wouldn't It Be Loverly?"	ELIZA and COSTERMONGERS
4. "With A Little Bit of Luck"	DOOLITTLE, HARRY and JAMIE
5. "I'm An Ordinary Man"	HIGGINS
6. "With A Little Bit of Luck" (Reprise)	DOOLITTLE and FRIENDS
7. "Just You Wait"	ELIZA
8. "The Rain in Spain"	HIGGINS, ELIZA and PICKERING
9. "I Could Have Danced All Night"	ELIZA, MRS. PEARCE and MAIDS
10. Ascot Gavotte	SPECTATORS AT THE RACE
11. "On the Street Where You Live"	FREDDY
12. "The Embassy Waltz"	HIGGINS, ELIZA, KARPATHY and GUESTS

Act Two

1. "You Did It"	HIGGINS, PICKERING, MRS. PEARCE and SERVANTS
2. "Just You Wait" (Reprise)	ELIZA

3. "On the Street Where FREDDY
　　You Live" (Reprise)
4. "Show Me" ELIZA and FREDDY
5. "Wouldn't It Be ELIZA and COSTERMONGERS
　　Loverly" (Reprise)
6. "Get Me to the Church DOOLITTLE, HARRY, JAMIE
　　on Time" 　　　　and COSTERMONGERS
7. "A Hymn to Him" HIGGINS
8. "Without You" HIGGINS and ELIZA
9. "I've Grown Accus- HIGGINS
　　tomed to Her Face"

Act One

The place is London, the time 1912.

Act Two

ACT ONE

Scene 1

Outside the Royal Opera House, Covent Garden.

Time: After theater, a cold March night.

At Rise: The opera is just over. Richly gowned, beautifully tailored Londoners are pouring from the Opera House and making their way across Covent Garden in search of taxis. Some huddle together under the columns of St. Paul's Church which are partially in view on one side of the stage. On the opposite side, there is a smudge-pot fire around which a quartet of costermongers are warming themselves. Calls of "Taxi" punctuate the icy air.

THREE STREET ENTERTAINERS, BUSKERS, *rush on to perform a few acrobatic tricks, stunts, and dance steps. They detain the crowd for a moment. The female member of the trio passes the hat as her two associates continue and reach the "climax" of their act.*

MRS. EYNSFORD-HILL, *a middle-aged lady in evening dress, and her son* FREDDY, *a young man of twenty, also in evening dress, come through the crowd in search of a taxi. One of the buskers collides into him. He is thrown backwards and strikes a figure hidden behind a group of people who now comes flying forward and lands in a heap. She is a flower girl,* ELIZA DOOLITTLE. *Her basket of flowers has been knocked from her hands and her violets scattered about. She is not at all an attractive person. She is perhaps eighteen, per-*

119

*haps twenty, hardly older. She wears a little sailor hat of
black straw that has long been exposed to the dust and
soot of London and has seldom if ever been brushed.
Her hair needs washing rather badly; its mousy color can
hardly be natural. She wears a shoddy shawl, a dirty
blouse with a coarse apron. Her boots are much the worse
for wear. She is no doubt as clean as she can afford to
be; but compared to the ladies she is very dirty. Her features are no worse than theirs; but their condition leaves
something to be desired, and she needs the services of
a dentist.*

ELIZA: Aaaooowww!

FREDDY (*clumsily trying to help her*): I'm frightfully
sorry.

ELIZA (*wailing*): Two bunches of violets trod in the
mud! A full day's wages. Why don't you look where
you're going?

MRS. EYNSFORD-HILL: Get a taxi, Freddy. Do you want
me to catch pneumonia?

FREDDY: I'm sorry, Mother. I'll get a taxi right away.
(*To* ELIZA) Sorry. (*He goes.*)

(COLONEL PICKERING *emerges dressed in evening clothes
and looking for a taxi. He is a middle-aged gentleman of
the amiable military type.*)

ELIZA (*to* MRS. EYNSFORD-HILL): Oh, he's your son, is
he? Well, if you'd done your duty by him as a mother
should, you wouldn't let him spoil a poor girl's flowers
and then run away without paying.

MRS. EYNSFORD-HILL: Go on about your business, my
girl. (*She follows her son.*)

ELIZA (*muttering to herself, as she collects her flowers*):
Two bunches of violets trod in the mud.

PICKERING (*calling off*): Taxi! Taxi!

ELIZA (*to* PICKERING): I say, Captain, buy a flower off
a poor girl.

PICKERING: I'm sorry. I haven't any change.

ELIZA: I can change half a crown. Here, take this for
tuppence.

PICKERING (*trying his pockets*): I really haven't any—
stop: here's three ha'pence, if that's any use to you.

ELIZA (*disappointed, but thinking three halfpence better
than nothing*): Thank you, sir.

A BYSTANDER (*to* ELIZA): Here, you be careful. Better
give him a flower fer it. There's a bloke there behind
the pillar taking down every blessed word you're
saying.

(*The* CROWD *turns to look behind the pillar.*)

ELIZA (*springing up terrified*): I ain't done nothin'
wrong by speakin' to the gentleman! I've a right to sell
flowers if I keep off the kerb. I'm a respectable girl; so
help me, I never spoke to him except to ask him to buy
a flower off me.

(*There is a general hubbub, mostly sympathetic to*
ELIZA, *but deprecating her excessive sensibility.*)

ANOTHER BYSTANDER: What's the row?

A HOXTON MAN: What's all the bloomin' noise?

A SELSEY MAN: There's a tec takin' her down.

ELIZA (*crying wildly—to* PICKERING): Oh, sir, don't let
him charge me! You dunno what it means to me. They'll
take away my character and drive me on the streets for
speakin' to gentlemen.

(PROFESSOR HIGGINS *pivots around the post and into
view.*)

HIGGINS: There! There! There! Who's hurting you, you
silly girl! What do you take me for?

ELIZA (*to* HIGGINS—*still hysterical*): On my Bible oath,
I never said a word. . . .

HIGGINS (*overbearing, but good-humored*): Oh, shut
up, shut up. Do I look like a policeman?

ELIZA: Then what did you take down my words for?
How do I know whether you took me down right? You
just show me what you wrote about me.

(HIGGINS *opens his book and holds it steadily under
her nose, though the pressure of the mob trying to read
it over his shoulders would upset a weaker man.*)
What's this? That ain't proper writing. I can't read that.

HIGGINS: I can. (*Reads, reproducing her pronunciation*) I say, Captain, buy a flower off a poor girl.

ELIZA: It's because I called him Captain! I meant no harm. (*To* PICKERING) Oh, sir, don't let him lay a charge agen me for a word like that. You . . .

PICKERING: Charge! I make no charge. (*To* HIGGINS) Really, sir, if you are a detective, you need not begin protecting me against molestation by young women until I ask you. Anybody could see the girl meant no harm.

THE SELSEY MAN: He ain't a tec. He's a gentleman. Look at his shoes.

HIGGINS (*turning on him genially*): And how are all your people down at Selsey?

THE SELSEY MAN (*suspiciously*): Who told you my people come from Selsey?

HIGGINS: Never mind. They did. (*To* ELIZA) How do you come to be up so far east? You were born in Lisson Grove.

ELIZA (*appalled*): Oooooh, what harm is there in my leaving Lisson Grove? It wasn't fit for a pig to live in; and I had to pay four-and-six a week. Oh, boo-hoo-oo—

HIGGINS: Live where you like; but stop that noise. (*With pad in hand, he becomes interested in the accents of the men grouped around the fire.*)

PICKERING (*to* ELIZA): Come, come! He can't touch you; you have a right to live where you please.

ELIZA (*subsiding into a brooding melancholy and talking very low-spiritedly to herself*): I'm a good girl, I am.

THE HOXTON MAN: Do you know where *I* come from?

HIGGINS (*promptly*): Hoxton.

THE HOXTON MAN (*amazed*): Well, who said I didn't! Blimey, you know everything, you do.

(*Titterings. Popular interest in the note-taker's performance increases.*)

ANOTHER BYSTANDER (*indicating* PICKERING): Tell him where he comes from, if you want to go fortunetelling.

HIGGINS: Cheltenham, Harrow, Cambridge and India.

PICKERING: Quite right.

AND STILL ANOTHER BYSTANDER: Blimey, he ain't a tec; he's a bloomin' busybody, that's what he is!

(*The crowd starts leaving, highly impressed.*)

PICKERING: May I ask, sir, do you do this sort of thing for a living on the music halls?

(*All have gone except the four* COSTERMONGERS *grouped about the smudge-pot fire,* HIGGINS, PICKERING, *and* ELIZA, *who is seated on the kerb against one of the pillars arranging her flowers and pitying herself in murmurs.*)

HIGGINS: I have thought of that. Perhaps I will someday.

ELIZA: He's no gentleman, he ain't, to interfere with a poor girl.

PICKERING: How do you do it, if I may ask?

HIGGINS: Simple phonetics. The science of speech. That's my profession, also my hobby. Anyone can spot an Irishman or a Yorkshireman by his brogue. I can place a man within six miles; I can place him within two miles in London. (*Indicating* ELIZA) Sometimes within two streets.

ELIZA: Ought to be ashamed of himself, unmanly coward!

PICKERING: But is there a living in that?

HIGGINS: Oh, yes. Quite a fat one.

ELIZA: Let him mind his own business and leave a poor girl—

HIGGINS (*explosively*): Woman! Cease this detestable boo-hooing instantly or else seek the shelter of some other place of worship.

ELIZA (*with feeble defiance*): I've a right to be here if I like, same as you.

HIGGINS: A woman who utters such depressing and disgusting sounds has no right to be anywhere—no right to live. Remember that you are a human being with a soul and the divine gift of articulate speech; that your native language is the language of Shakespeare and Milton and the Bible; and don't sit there crooning like a bilious pigeon.

ELIZA (*quite overwhelmed, looking up at him in mingled wonder and deprecation without daring to raise her head*): Aoooooooooooow!

HIGGINS:

Look at her—a pris'ner of the gutters;
Condemned by ev'ry syllable she utters.
By right she should be taken out and hung
For the cold-blooded murder of the English tongue!

ELIZA: A-o-o-o-w!

HIGGINS (*imitating her*): Aoooow! Heavens, what a noise!

This is what the British population
Calls an element'ry education.

PICKERING: Come, sir, I think you picked a poor example.

HIGGINS: Did I?

Hear them down in Soho Square
Dropping aitches everywhere,
Speaking English any way they like.

(*To one of the* COSTERMONGERS *at the fire*) You, sir, did you go to school?

COSTERMONGER: Whatya tike me fer, a fool?

HIGGINS (*to* PICKERING):

No one taught him "take" instead of "tike."
Hear a Yorkshireman, or worse,
Hear a Cornishman converse.
I'd rather hear a choir singing flat.
Chickens cackling in a barn . . .

(*Pointing to* ELIZA)

Just like this one—!

ELIZA: —Garn!
HIGGINS:

I ask you, sir, what sort of word is that?
It's "Aooow" and "Garn" that keep her in her place.
Not her wretched clothes and dirty face.

Why can't the English teach their children how to speak?
This verbal class distinction by now should be antique.
If you spoke as she does, sir,
Instead of the way you do,
Why, you might be selling flowers, too.

PICKERING: I beg your pardon!
HIGGINS:

An Englishman's way of speaking absolutely classifies him
The moment he talks he makes some other Englishman despise him.
One common language I'm afraid we'll never get.
Oh, why can't the English learn to set
A good example to people whose English is painful to your ears?
The Scotch and the Irish leave you close to tears.

There even are places where English completely disappears.
In America, they haven't used it for years!
Why can't the English teach their children how to speak?
Norwegians learn Norwegian; the Greeks are taught their Greek.
In France every Frenchman knows his language from "A" to "Zed"
The French never care what they do, actually, as long as they pronounce it properly.

Arabians learn Arabian with the speed of summer
lightning.
The Hebrews learn it backwards, which is absolutely
frightening.
But use proper English, you're regarded as a freak.
Why can't the English,
Why can't the English learn to speak?

(*He looks thoughtfully at* ELIZA.) You see this creature
with her kerbstone English; the English that will
keep her in the gutter to the end of her days? Well,
sir, in six months I could pass her off as a duchess at
an Embassy ball. I could even get her a place as a
lady's maid or shop assistant, which requires better
English.

ELIZA (*rising with sudden interest*): Here, what's that
you say?

HIGGINS: Yes, you squashed cabbage leaf, you disgrace
to the noble architecture of these columns, you incarnate
insult to the English language; I could pass you off as
the Queen of Sheba.

PICKERING (*interested in* HIGGINS *but more so in finding
a taxi, thinks he sees one and moves quickly to hail it*):
Taxi!

ELIZA: Aooow! (*To* PICKERING) You don't believe
that, Captain?

PICKERING: Taxi! (*He loses the cab and comes back.*)
Oh, well, anything is possible. I myself am a student of
Indian dialects.

HIGGINS (*eagerly*): Are you? Do you know Colonel
Pickering, the author of *Spoken Sanskrit?*

PICKERING: I am Colonel Pickering. Who are you?

HIGGINS: Henry Higgins, author of *Higgins' Universal
Alphabet.*

PICKERING (*amazed*): I came from India to meet you!

HIGGINS (*with enthusiasm*): I was going to India to
meet you!

PICKERING (*extending his hand*): Higgins!

HIGGINS (*extending his*): Pickering! (*They shake hands.*)
Where are you staying?

PICKERING: At the Carleton.

HIGGINS: No, you're not. You're staying at 27-A Wimpole
Street. Come with me and we'll have a jaw over supper.

PICKERING: Right you are.

(*They start off together.*)

ELIZA (*to* HIGGINS *as they pass her*): Buy a flower, kind
sir. I'm short for my lodging.

HIGGINS (*shocked at the girl's mendacity*): Liar! You
said you could change half a crown.

ELIZA (*in desperation*): You ought to be stuffed with
nails, you ought. Here! (*Shoving her basket at him*) Take
the whole bloomin' basket for sixpence!

(*The church clock strikes the second quarter.*)

HIGGINS (*he raises his hat solemnly*): Ah. The church.
A reminder. (*Throws a handful of money into the basket
and follows* PICKERING) Indian dialects have always fascinated me. I have records of over fifty.

PICKERING: Have you, now. Did you know there are
over two hundred?

HIGGINS: By George, it's worse than London. Do you
know them all?

(*They disappear down the street.*)

ELIZA (*picking up a half crown*): Ah-ow-ooh! (*Picking
up a couple of florins*) Aah-ow-ooh! (*Picking up several
coins*) Aaaaaaa-ow-ooh! (*Picking up a half sovereign*)
Aaaaaaaaaaah-ow-ooh!! (*She skips to the fire to display
her wealth.*)

FIRST COSTERMONGER (*with a sweep of his hat*): Shouldn't
you stand up, gentlemen? We've got a bloomin' heiress
in our midst!

SECOND COSTERMONGER (*rises and clicking heels*):
Would you be lookin' for a good butler, Eliza?

ELIZA (*haughtily*): You won't do. (*She walks away.*)

SECOND COSTERMONGER:

It's rather dull in town,
I think I'll take me to Paree.

THIRD COSTERMONGER:

> The missus wants to open up,
> The castle in Capri!

FIRST COSTERMONGER:

> Me doctor recommends
> A quiet summer by the sea.

THE FOUR:

> Mmmmmmmm! Mmmmmmm!
> Wouldn't it be loverly!

THIRD COCKNEY: Where're ya bound for this spring, Eliza? Biarritz?

ELIZA (*leaning against the pillar*):

> All I want is a room somewhere,
> Far away from the cold night air;
> With one enormous chair . . .
> Oh, wouldn't it be loverly?

> Lots of choc'late for me to eat;
> Lots of coal makin' lots of heat;
> Warm face, warm hands, warm feet . . . !
> Oh, wouldn't it be loverly?

> Oh, so loverly sittin' absobloominlutely still
> I would never budge till spring
> Crept over me winder sill.

> Someone's head restin' on my knee,
> Warm and tender as he can be,
> Who takes good care of me . . .
> Oh, wouldn't it be loverly?
> Loverly! Loverly!
> Loverly! Loverly!

(*As* ELIZA *spins out her daydream, a few other* FLOWER GIRLS *and* VENDERS *are drawn on and stand silently listening. When she finishes, the four at the fire beguiled into the mood repeat the refrain as* ELIZA *and the others act out a dinner in an expensive restaurant: the ordering, the wine, the food—and riding home in a taxi afterwards. A dustcart serves the purpose. An icy blast blows across the market place bringing them quickly back to reality and they all gather around the fire and warm their hands.*)

Scene 2

Tenement section, Tottenham Court Road. A shabby back alley filled with atmosphere for everyone but those who live there. There is a small public house on one side of the stage, a converted mews on the other and, rising in the end of the street that divides the two, the misty outline of St. Paul's Cathedral (Chris Wren's, not the Covent Garden St. Paul's).

Time: Later that evening.

There is a commotion at the pub. GEORGE, *the bartender, is discovered forcibly evicting two disorderly members of the lowest possible class, by the name* HARRY *and* JAMIE. GEORGE *now directs his remarks into the bar.*

BARTENDER: I ain't runnin' no charity bazaar. Drinks is to be paid for or not drunk. Come on, Doolittle. Out you go. Hop it now, Doolittle. On the double. On the double.

(ALFRED DOOLITTLE *emerges. He is an elderly but vigorous dustman, clad in the costume of his profession, including a hat with a black brim covering his neck and shoulders. He has well marked and rather interesting features, and seems equally free from fear and conscience. He has a remarkably expressive voice, the result of a habit of giving vent to his feelings without reserve. His present pose is that of wounded honor and casual disdain.*)

DOOLITTLE: Thanks for your hospitality, George. Send the bill to Buckingham Palace. (*The* BARTENDER *exits into pub as* DOOLITTLE *joins his associates.*) Hyde Park to walk through on a fine spring night; the whole ruddy city of London to roam about in sellin' her bloomin' flowers. I give her all that, and then I disappears and leaves her on her own to enjoy it. Now if that ain't worth half a crown now and again, I'll take off my belt and give her what for.

JAMIE: You got a good heart, Alfie, but if you want that half a crown from Eliza, you better have a good story to go with it.

(ELIZA *ambles on.*)

DOOLITTLE (*with paternal joy*): Eliza! What a surprise!

ELIZA (*walking past him*): Not a brass farthing.

DOOLITTLE (*grabbing her arm*): Now you look here, Eliza. You wouldn't have the heart to send me home to your stepmother without a bit of liquid protection, now would you?

ELIZA: Stepmother. Ha! Stepmother, indeed!

DOOLITTLE: Well, I'm willing to marry her. It's me that suffers by it. I'm a slave to that woman, Eliza. Just because I ain't her lawful husband. (*Lovably*) Come on, Eliza, slip your old dad half a crown to go home on.

ELIZA (*taking a coin from her basket, flipping it in air and catching it*): Well, I had a bit of luck meself tonight. So here. (*Gives him coin.*)

HARRY (*jubilantly calls into pub*): George! Three glorious beers!

ELIZA: But don't kccp comin' around countin' on half crowns from me! (*She disappears into the converted mews.*)

DOOLITTLE: Goodnight, Eliza! You're a noble daughter! (*He turns to his friends smugly.*) You see, boys, I told you not to go home! It's just Faith, Hope, and a little bit of luck!

The Lord above gave man an arm of iron
So he could do his job and never shirk.

The Lord above gave man an arm of iron—but
With a little bit of luck,
With a little bit of luck,
Someone else'll do the blinkin' work!

THE THREE:

With a little bit . . . with a little bit. . . .
With a little bit of luck
You'll never work!

DOOLITTLE:

The Lord above made liquor for temptation,
To see if man could turn away from sin.
The Lord above made liquor for temptation—but
With a little bit of luck,
With a little bit of luck,
When temptation comes you'll give right in!

THE THREE:

With a little bit. . . . with a little bit. . . .
With a little bit of luck,
You'll give right in.

DOOLITTLE:

Oh, you can walk the straight and narrow;
But with a little bit of luck
You'll run amuck!

The gentle sex was made for man to marry,
To share his nest and see his food is cooked.
The gentle sex was made for man to marry—but
With a little bit of luck,
With a little bit of luck,
You can have it all and not get hooked.

THE THREE:

> With a little bit. . . . with a little bit. . . .
> With a little bit of luck
> You won't get hooked.
> With a little bit. . . . with a little bit. . . .
> With a little bit of bloomin' luck!

(*An* ANGRY WOMAN *pokes her head out of the upstairs window of the mews.*)

ANGRY WOMAN: Shut your face down there! How's a woman supposed to get her rest?

DOOLITTLE: I'm tryin' to keep 'em quiet, lady!

(*The voice of an* ANGRY MAN *is heard down the street.*)

ANGRY MAN: Shut up! Once and for all, shut up!

ANOTHER ANGRY MAN: One more sound, so help me, I'll call a copper!

DOOLITTLE: Here, here, here! Stop that loud talk! People are tryin' to sleep! (*He turns to his friends.*) Let's try to be neighborly-like, boys. After all . . .

> (*Sings softly*)
> The Lord above made man to help his neighbor,
> No matter where, on land, or sea, or foam.
> The Lord above made man to help his neighbor—but
> With a little bit of luck,
> With a little bit of luck,
> When he comes around you won't be home!

JAMIE *and* HARRY:

> With a little bit. . . . with a little bit. . . .
> With a little bit of luck,
> You won't be home.

DOOLITTLE:

> They're always throwin' goodness at you;
> But with a little bit of luck

A man can duck!
Oh, it's a crime for man to go philanderin'
And fill his wife's poor heart with grief and doubt.
Oh, it's a crime for man to go philanderin'—but
With a little bit of luck,
With a little bit of luck,
You can see the bloodhound don't find out!

THE THREE (*at the top of their lungs*):

With a little bit. . . . with a little bit. . . .
With a little bit of luck
She won't find out!
With a little bit. . . . with a little bit. . . .
With a little bit of bloomin' luck!

(*Angry cries descend on them from all over the neighborhood. They cheerfully disregard them and re-enter the pub.*)

Scene 3

HIGGINS' *study in Wimpole Street.*
It is a room on the first floor with one window in an alcove looking out on the street and double doors in the middle of the back wall. There is a balcony above them with stairs to one side leading up to it. There is another door on the balcony and the wall of the balcony is entirely covered with bookcases. Next to the door is a small table upon which is a recording machine and speaker horn.
There is a desk below the alcove upon which is a small bust of Plato, a mass of papers, several tuning forks of different sizes, and a telephone. Next to the desk is a small xylophone and another recorder and speaker. The alcove behind is a mass of filing cabinets and books. There is a bird cage containing a bird next to the window.
There is a sofa in the middle of the room, an easy chair next to the stairs and a small stool in front of the desk.

Behind the easy chair is another recording machine and, against the wall by the double doors, still another.

Time: The next day.

The room is dark. In the darkness between the scenes strange guttural sounds pour forth from the public address system. PICKERING *is seated in the easy chair.* HIGGINS *is standing by the recording machine next to his desk. The strange sounds heard in the darkness a moment before are now discovered to be coming from the recorder. When the lights go on, as they will in a moment,* HIGGINS *in the morning light is seen to be a robust, vital, appetizing sort of man of forty or thereabouts. He is of the energetic scientific type, heartily, even violently, interested in everything that can be studied as a scientific subject, and careless about himself and other people, including their feelings. He is, in fact, but for his years and size, rather like a very impetuous baby "taking notice" eagerly and loudly, and requiring almost as much watching to keep him out of unintended mischief. His manner varies from genial bullying when he is in a good humor to stormy petulance when anything goes wrong; but he is so entirely frank and void of malice that he remains likable even in his least reasonable moments.*

PICKERING: I say, Higgins, couldn't we turn on the lights?

HIGGINS: Nonsense, you hear much better in the dark.

PICKERING: But it's a fearful strain listening to all these vowel sounds. I'm quite done up for this morning.

(MRS. PEARCE *enters. She is* HIGGINS' *housekeeper.*)

MRS. PEARCE: Mr. Higgins, are you there?

HIGGINS: What is it, Mrs. Pearce? (*He turns down the volume of the machine.*)

MRS. PEARCE: A young woman wants to see you, sir.

HIGGINS (*turning the machine off*): A young woman! What does she want? (*He switches on the light.*) Has she an interesting accent? (*To* PICKERING) Let's have her up. Show her up, Mrs. Pearce.

MRS. PEARCE: Very well, sir. It's for you to say. (*She goes out into the hall.*)

HIGGINS: This is rather a bit of luck. I'll show you how I make records. We'll set her talking; and I'll take her down in Bell's Visible Speech; then in Broad Romic; and then we'll get her on the phonograph so that you can turn her on as often as you like with the written transcript before you.

MRS. PEARCE (*returning*): This is the young woman, sir.

(ELIZA *enters in state. She has a hat with three ostrich feathers, orange, sky-blue, and red. She has a nearly clean apron, and the shoddy coat has been tidied a little. The pathos of this deplorable figure, with its innocent vanity and consequential air, touches* PICKERING, *who has already straightened himself in the presence of* MRS. PEARCE. *But as to* HIGGINS, *the only distinction he makes between men and women is that when he is neither bullying nor exclaiming to the heavens against some featherweight cross, he coaxes women as a child coaxes its nurse when it wants to get anything out of her.*)

HIGGINS (*brusquely, recognizing her with unconcealed disappointment, and at once, babylike, making an intolerable grievance of it*): Why, this is the girl I jotted down last night. She's no use: I've got all the records I want of the Lisson Grove lingo, and I'm not going to waste another cylinder on it. (*To the girl*) Be off with you: I don't want you.

ELIZA: Don't be so saucy. You ain't heard what I come for yet. (*To* MRS. PEARCE, *who is waiting at the door for further instructions*) Did you tell him I come in a taxi?

MRS. PEARCE: Nonsense, girl! What do you think a gentleman like Mr. Higgins cares what you came in?

ELIZA: Oh, we are proud! He ain't above giving lessons, not him: I heard him say so. Well, I ain't come here to ask for any compliment; and if my money's not good enough I can go elsewhere.

HIGGINS: Good enough for what?

ELIZA: Good enough for ye-oo. Now you know, don't

you? I'm come to have lessons, I am. And to pay for 'em too: make no mistake.

HIGGINS (*stunned*): Well!!! (*Recovering his breath with a gasp*) What do you expect me to say to you?

ELIZA: Well, if you was a gentleman, you might ask me to sit down, I think. Don't I tell you I'm bringing you business?

HIGGINS: Pickering, shall we ask this baggage to sit down, or shall we throw her out of the window?

ELIZA (*running away in terror*): Ah-ah-oh-ow-ow-ow-oo! (*Wounded and whimpering*) I won't be called a baggage when I've offered to pay like any lady!

PICKERING (*gently*): What is it you want, my girl?

ELIZA: I want to be a lady in a flower shop stead of selling at the corner of Tottenham Court Road. But they won't take me unless I can talk more genteel. He said he could teach me. Well, here I am ready to pay him—not asking any favor—and he treats me as if I was dirt. I know what lessons cost as well as you do; and I'm ready to pay.

HIGGINS: How much?

ELIZA (*coming back to him, triumphant*): Now you're talking! I thought you'd come off it when you saw a chance of getting back a bit of what you chucked at me last night. (*Confidentially*) You'd had a drop in, hadn't you?

HIGGINS (*peremptorily*): Sit down.

ELIZA: Oh, if you're going to make a compliment of it—

HIGGINS (*thundering at her*): Sit down.

MRS. PEARCE (*severely*): Sit down, girl. Do as you're told.

PICKERING (*gently*): What is your name?

ELIZA: Eliza Doolittle.

PICKERING: Won't you sit down, Miss Doolittle?

ELIZA (*coyly*): Oh, I don't mind if I do. (*She sits down on sofa.*)

HIGGINS: How much do you propose to pay me for the lessons?

ELIZA: Oh, I know what's right. A lady friend of mine gets French lessons for heighteen pence an hour from a real French gentleman. Well, you wouldn't have the face to ask me the same for teaching me my own language as you would for French; so I won't give more than a shilling. Take it or leave it.

HIGGINS: You know, Pickering, if you consider a shilling, not as a simple shilling, but as a percentage of this girl's income, it works out as fully equivalent to sixty or seventy pounds from a millionaire. By George, it's the biggest offer I ever had.

ELIZA (*rising, terrified*): Sixty pounds! What are you talkin' about? I never offered you sixty pounds! Where would I get . . .

HIGGINS: Oh, hold your tongue.

ELIZA (*weeping*): But I ain't got sixty pounds. Oh . . .

MRS. PEARCE: Don't cry, you silly girl. Sit down. Nobody is going to touch your money.

HIGGINS: Somebody is going to touch you with a broomstick, if you don't stop snivelling. Now, sit down.

ELIZA: Aoooow! One would think you was my father!

HIGGINS: If I decide to teach you, I'll be worse than two fathers to you. Here— (*He offers her his silk handkerchief.*)

ELIZA: What's this for?

HIGGINS: To wipe your eyes. To wipe any part of your face that feels moist. Remember, that's your handkerchief; and that's your sleeve. Don't mistake the one for the other if you wish to become a lady in a shop.

PICKERING: Higgins, I'm interested. What about your boast that you could pass her off as a duchess at the Embassy Ball? I'll say you're the greatest teacher alive if you can make that good. I'll bet you all the expenses of the experiment you can't do it. And I'll even pay for the lessons.

ELIZA: Oh, you're real good. Thank you, Captain.

HIGGINS (*tempted, looking at her*): It's almost irresistible. She's so deliciously low—so horribly dirty!

ELIZA: Aoooow! I ain't dirty: I washed my face and hands afore I come, I did.

HIGGINS: I'll take it! I'll make a duchess of this draggle-tailed guttersnipe!

ELIZA: Aoooooooow!

HIGGINS (*carried away*): I'll start today! Now! This moment! Take her away and clean her, Mrs. Pearce. Sandpaper if it won't come off any other way. Is there a good fire in the kitchen?

MRS. PEARCE: Yes, but—

HIGGINS (*storming on*): Take all her clothes off and burn them. Ring up and order some new ones. Wrap her up in brown paper till they come.

ELIZA: You're no gentleman, you're not, to talk of such things. I'm a good girl, I am; and I know what the likes of you are, I do.

HIGGINS: We want none of your slum prudery here, young woman. You've got to learn to behave like a duchess. Take her away, Mrs. Pearce. If she gives you any trouble, wallop her.

ELIZA: I'll call the police, I will!

MRS. PEARCE: But I've got no place to put her.

HIGGINS: Put her in the dustbin.

ELIZA: Aooooow!

PICKERING: Oh come, Higgins! Be reasonable.

MRS. PEARCE: You must be reasonable, Mr. Higgins, really you must. You can't walk over everybody like this.

(HIGGINS *thus scolded subsides. The hurricane is succeeded by a zephyr of amiable surprise.*)

HIGGINS (*with professional exquisiteness of modulation*): I walk over everybody? My dear Mrs. Pearce, my dear Pickering. I never had the slightest intention of walking over anybody. All I propose is that we should be kind to this poor girl. If I did not express myself clearly it was because I did not wish to hurt her delicacy, or yours.

MRS. PEARCE: But, sir, you can't take a girl up like that as if you were picking up a pebble on the beach.

HIGGINS: Why not?

MRS. PEARCE: Why not? But you don't know anything

about her! What about her parents? She may be married.

ELIZA: Garn!

HIGGINS: There! As the girl very properly says: Garn!

ELIZA: Who'd marry me?

HIGGINS (*suddenly resorting to the most thrillingly beautiful low tones in his best elocutionary style*): By George, Eliza, the streets will be strewn with the bodies of men shooting themselves for your sake before I've done with you.

ELIZA: Here! I'm goin' away! He's off his chump, he is. I don't want no balmies teachin' me.

HIGGINS (*wounded in his tenderest point by her insensibility to his elocution*): Oh, indeed! I'm mad, am I? Very well, Mrs. Pearce, you needn't order the new clothes for her. Throw her out! (*He deftly retrieves his handkerchief.*)

MRS. PEARCE: Stop, Mr. Higgins! I won't allow it. Go home to your parents, girl.

ELIZA: I ain't got no parents.

HIGGINS: There you are. "She ain't got no parents." What's all the fuss about? The girl doesn't belong to anybody, and she's no use to anybody but me. Take her upstairs and—

MRS. PEARCE: But what's to become of her? Is she to be paid anything? Oh, do be sensible, sir.

HIGGINS (*impatiently*): What on earth will she want with money? She'll have her food and her clothes. She'll only drink if you give her money.

ELIZA (*turning on him*): Oh, you are a brute. It's a lie; nobody ever saw the sign of liquor on me. (*To* PICKERING) Oh, sir, you're a gentleman; don't let him speak to me like that!

PICKERING (*in good-humored remonstrance*): Does it occur to you, Higgins, that the girl has some feelings?

HIGGINS (*looking critically at her*): Oh, no, I don't think so. Not any feelings that we need bother about. (*Cheerily*) Have you, Eliza?

MRS. PEARCE: Mr. Higgins. I must know on what terms the girl is to be here. What is to become of her when you've finished your teaching? You must look ahead a little, sir.

HIGGINS: What's to become of her if I leave her in the gutter? Answer me that, Mrs. Pearce.

MRS. PEARCE: That's her own business, not yours, Mr. Higgins.

HIGGINS: Well, when I've done with her, we can throw her back into the gutter, and then it will be her own business again; so that's all right. (*He is moved to a chuckle by his own little pleasantry.*)

ELIZA: Oh, you've no feelin' heart in you: you don't care for nothing but yourself. Here! I've had enough of this. I'm going. (*She makes for the door.*)

HIGGINS (*taking her by the arm*): Eliza! (*Snatching a chocolate cream from the table, his eyes suddenly twinkling with mischief*) Have some chocolates.

ELIZA (*halting, tempted*): How do I know what might be in them? I've heard of girls being drugged by the like of you.

(HIGGINS *breaks the chocolate in two, puts one half into his mouth and bolts it.*)

HIGGINS: Pledge of good faith, Eliza. I eat one half and you eat the other. (ELIZA *opens her mouth to retort.* HIGGINS *pops the chocolate into it.*) You shall have boxes of them, barrels of them, every day. You shall live on them, eh?

ELIZA (*her mouth full*): I wouldn't have ate it, only I'm too ladylike to take it out of me mouth.

HIGGINS (*taking her by the hand and leading her up the stairs*): Think of it, Eliza. Think of chocolates, and taxis, and gold, and diamonds. (*They reach the balcony.*)

ELIZA: No! I don't want no gold and no diamonds. I'm a good girl, I am.

PICKERING: Excuse me, Higgins, but I really must interfere! Mrs. Pearce is quite right. If this girl is to put herself in your hands for six months for an experiment in teaching, she must understand thoroughly what she's doing!

HIGGINS (*impressed with* PICKERING'S *logic, considers for a moment*): Eliza, you are to stay here for the next six months learning how to speak beautifully, like a lady in a florist's shop. If you're good and do whatever you're told, you shall sleep in a proper bedroom and have lots to eat, and money to buy chocolates and take rides in taxis. If you're naughty and idle you will sleep in the back kitchen among the black beetles, and be walloped by Mrs. Pearce with a broomstick. At the end of six months you shall go to Buckingham Palace in a carriage, beautifully dressed. If the King finds out you're not a lady, you will be taken by the police to the Tower of London where your head will be cut off as a warning to other presumptuous flower girls. If you are not found out, you shall have a present of seven-and-six to start life with as a lady in a shop. If you refuse this offer you will be the most ungrateful, wicked girl; and the angels will weep for you. (*To* PICKERING) Now are you satisfied, Pickering? (*To* MRS. PEARCE) Could I put it more plainly or fairly, Mrs. Pearce?

MRS. PEARCE (*resigned, starts up the stairs*): Come with me, Eliza.

HIGGINS: That's right, Mrs. Pearce. Bundle her off to the bathroom.

ELIZA (*reluctantly and suspiciously*): You're a great bully, you are. I won't stay here if I don't like. And I won't let nobody wallop me.

MRS. PEARCE: Don't answer back, girl. (*She leads* ELIZA *through the door.*)

ELIZA (*as she goes*): If I'd known what I was lettin' myself in for, I wouldn't have come up here. I've always been a good girl and I won't be put upon . . . (*She follows* MRS. PEARCE *out the door.*)

HIGGINS (*coming down the stairs*): In six months—in three if she has a good ear and a quick tongue—I'll take her anywhere and pass her off as anything. I'll make a queen of that barbarous wretch.

PICKERING: Higgins, forgive the bluntness, but if I'm to be in this business, I shall feel responsible for the girl.

I hope it's clearly understood that no advantage is to be taken of her position.

HIGGINS: What? That thing? Sacred, I assure you.

PICKERING (*gravely*): Now come, Higgins, you know what I mean! This is no trifling matter! Are you a man of good character where women are concerned?

HIGGINS: Have you ever met a man of good character where women were concerned?

PICKERING: Yes. Very frequently.

HIGGINS (*dogmatically*): Well, I haven't. I find that the moment I let a woman make friends with me she becomes jealous, exacting, suspicious and a damned nuisance. I find that the moment I let myself become friends with a woman, I become selfish and tyrannical. So here I am, a confirmed old bachelor, and likely to remain so. After all, Pickering . . .

> I'm an ordinary man;
> Who desires nothing more
> Than just the ordinary chance
> To live exactly as he likes
> And do precisely what he wants.
> An average man am I
> Of no eccentric whim;
> Who likes to live his life
> Free of strife,
> Doing whatever he thinks is best for him.
> Just an ordinary man.
>
> But let a woman in your life
> And your serenity is through!
> She'll redecorate your home
> From the cellar to the dome;
> Then get on to the enthralling
> Fun of overhauling
> You.
>
> Oh, let a woman in your life
> And you are up against the wall!

Make a plan and you will find
She has something else in mind;
And so rather than do either
You do something else that neither
Likes at all.

You want to talk of Keats or Milton;
She only wants to talk of love.
You go to see a play or ballet,
And spend it searching for her glove.

Oh, let a woman in your life
And you invite eternal strife!
Let them buy their wedding bands
For those anxious little hands;
I'd be equally as willing
For a dentist to be drilling
Than to ever let a woman in my life!

(*With sudden amiability*)

I'm a very gentle man;
Even-tempered and good-natured,
Whom you never hear complain;
Who has the milk of human kindness
By the quart in ev'ry vein.
A patient man am I
Down to my fingertips;
The sort who never could,
Ever would,
Let an insulting remark escape his lips.

(*Violently*)

But let a woman in your life
And patience hasn't got a chance.
She will beg you for advice;
Your reply will be concise.
And she'll listen very nicely

Then go out and do precisely
What she wants!
You were a man of grace and polish
Who never spoke above a hush.
Now all at once you're using language
That would make a sailor blush.

Oh, let a woman in your life
And you are plunging in a knife!
Let the others of my sex
Tie the knot—around their necks;
I'd prefer a new edition
Of the Spanish Inquisition
Than to ever let a woman in my life!

(The storm over, he "cheeps" sweetly to the bird.)

I'm a quiet living man
Who prefers to spend his evenings
In the silence of his room;
Who likes an atmosphere as restful
As an undiscovered tomb.
A pensive man am I
Of philosophic joys;
Who likes to meditate,
Contemplate,
Free from humanity's mad, inhuman noise.
Just a quiet living man.

(With abrupt rage)

But let a woman in your life
And your sabbatical is through!
In a line that never ends
Come an army of her friends;
Come to jabber and to chatter
And to tell her what the matter
Is with you.

She'll have a booming, boist'rous fam'ly
Who will descend on you en masse.
She'll have a large Wagnerian mother
With a voice that shatters glass!

Oh, let a woman in your life . . .

(*He turns on one of the machines at the accelerated speed so that the voice coming over the speaker becomes a piercing female babble. He runs to the next machine.*)

Let a woman in your life . . .

(*He turns it on the same way and dashes to the next.*)

Let a woman in your life . . .

(*He turns on the third; the third being the master control, he slowly turns the volume up until the chattering is unbearable.* PICKERING *covers his ears, his face knotted in pain. Having illustrated his point,* HIGGINS *suddenly turns all the machines off and makes himself comfortable in a chair.*)

I shall never let a woman in my life!

(*The lights black out for the end of the scene.*)

Scene 4

The tenement section, Tottenham Court Road, the same as Act One, Scene 2.

Time: Noon, three days later.

At Rise: MRS. HOPKINS, *a disheveled Cockney lady, has*

been imparting some juicy gossip to a group of delighted neighbors. She is holding a bird cage and a Chinese fan.

MRS. HOPKINS: How'd ya like that? Knocked me fer a row of pins, it did.

(GEORGE, *the bartender, forcibly evicts* HARRY *and* JAMIE *and then calls into the pub.*)

GEORGE: Come on, Doolittle. Out you go. Hop it now. I ain't runnin' no charity bazaar.

DOOLITTLE (*coming from the pub*): Thanks for your hospitality, George. Send . . .

GEORGE: Yes, I know. Send the bill to Buckingham Palace. (*He goes back into the pub.*)

MRS. HOPKINS: You can buy your own drinks now, Alfie Doolittle. Fallen into a tub of butter, you have.

DOOLITTLE: What tub of butter?

MRS. HOPKINS: Your daughter, Eliza. Oh, you're a lucky man, Alfie Doolittle.

DOOLITTLE: What are you talkin' about? What about Eliza?

MRS. HOPKINS (*to the crowd*): He don't know. Her own father, and he don't know. (*She and her friends have a good laugh at this.*) Moved in with a swell, Eliza has. Left here in a taxi all by herself, smart as paint, and ain't been home for three days. And then I gets a message from her this morning: she wants her things sent over to 27-A Wimpole Street, care of Professor Higgins. And what things does she want? Her bird cage, and her Chinese fan. (*She hands them to* DOOLITTLE.) But, she says, never mind about sendin' any clothes! (*She, her friends and* HARRY *and* JAMIE *laugh uproariously.* DOOLITTLE'S *face shines with paternal pride and the prospect of prosperous days.*)

DOOLITTLE: I knowed she had a career in front of her! Harry, boy, we're in for a booze-up. The sun is shinin' on Alfred P. Doolittle!

> A man was made to help support his children,
> Which is the right and proper thing to do.
> A man was made to help support his children—but

With a little bit of luck,
With a little bit of luck,
They'll go out and start supporting you!

ALL:

With a little bit . . . with a little bit . . .
With a little bit of luck,
They'll work for you.

He doesn't have a tuppence in his pocket.
The poorest bloke you'll ever hope to meet.
He doesn't have a tuppence in his pocket—but
With a little bit of luck,
With a little bit of luck,
Hell be movin' up to easy street.

With a little bit . . . with a little bit . . .
With a little bit of luck,
He's movin' up.
With a little bit . . . with a little bit . . .
With a little bit of bloomin' luck!

(*To the cheers of the crowd,* DOOLITTLE *trips gaily off, a man on the way to El Dorado.*)

Scene 5

HIGGINS' *study.*

Time: Later that afternoon.

At Rise: PICKERING *is seated in the wing chair, reading his paper.* MRS. PEARCE *is standing near the desk holding some letters in her hand.* HIGGINS *is on the balcony engrossed in a bit of research.*

MRS. PEARCE (*sternly*): Mr. Higgins, you simply cannot go on working the girl this way. Making her say her alphabet over and over, from sunup to sundown, even during meals—when will it stop?

HIGGINS (*detached but still logical*): When she does it properly, of course. Is that all, Mrs. Pearce?

MRS. PEARCE: No, sir. The mail.

HIGGINS: Pay the bills and say no to the invitations.

MRS. PEARCE: There's another letter from that American millionaire, Ezra D. Wallingford. He still wants you to lecture for his Moral Reform League.

HIGGINS: Throw it away.

MRS. PEARCE (*not to be put off*): It's the third letter he's written you, sir. You should at least answer it.

HIGGINS (*anything for peace*): Oh, all right. Leave it on the desk. I'll get to it.

(MRS. PEARCE *places the letter on the desk. While she is doing so, the* BUTLER *enters and addresses* HIGGINS *on the landing.*)

BUTLER: If you please, sir, there's a dustman downstairs, Alfred Doolittle, who wants to see you. He says you have his daughter here.

PICKERING (*coming to life*): Phew! I say!

HIGGINS (*promptly*): Send the blackguard up. (*The* BUTLER *goes.*)

PICKERING: He may not be a blackguard, Higgins.

HIGGINS: Nonsense. Of course he's a blackguard.

PICKERING: Whether he is or not, I'm afraid we shall have some trouble with him.

HIGGINS (*confidently*): Oh no, I think not. If there's any trouble he shall have it with me, not I with him.

(*The* BUTLER *returns.*)

BUTLER: Doolittle, sir.

(DOOLITTLE *enters and gravely addresses* PICKERING.)

DOOLITTLE: Professor 'iggins?

(*The* BUTLER *goes.*)

HIGGINS (*from the balcony*): Here!

(DOOLITTLE *looks up, momentarily shaken.*)

DOOLITTLE: Morning, Governor. I come about a very serious matter, Governor.

HIGGINS (*to* PICKERING): Born in Hounslow, mother Welsh! (*To* DOOLITTLE) What do you want, Doolittle?

DOOLITTLE (*menacingly*): I want my daughter. That's what I want. See?

HIGGINS: Of course you do. You're her father, aren't you? I'm glad to see you have some spark of family feeling left. She's upstairs, here. Take her away at once.

DOOLITTLE (*fearfully taken aback*): What??!!

HIGGINS: Take her away. Do you suppose I'm going to keep your daughter for you?

DOOLITTLE (*remonstrating*): Now, now, look here, Governor. Is this reasonable? Is it fairity to take advantage of a man like this? The girl belongs to me. You got her. Where do I come in?

HIGGINS (*charging down the stairs*): How dare you come here and attempt to blackmail me? You sent her here on purpose.

DOOLITTLE (*protesting*): Now don't take a man up like that, Governor.

HIGGINS: The police shall take you up. This is a plant—a plot to extort money by threats. I shall telephone the police.

(*He goes resolutely to the telephone on the desk.*)

DOOLITTLE: Have I asked you for a brass farthing? I leave it to this gentleman here. (*To* PICKERING) Have I said a word about money?

HIGGINS: What else did you come for?

DOOLITTLE (*sweetly*): Well, what would a man come for? Be human, Governor. (*He wheezes genially in* HIGGINS' *face and rocks him back several paces.*)

HIGGINS (*recovering*): Alfred, you sent her here on purpose?

DOOLITTLE: So help me, Governor, I never did.

HIGGINS: Then how did you know she was here?

DOOLITTLE: I'll tell ya, Governor, if you'll only let me get a word in. I'm willing to tell ya. I'm wanting to tell ya. I'm waiting to tell ya.

HIGGINS: Pickering, this chap has a certain natural gift

of rhetoric. Observe the rhythm of his native woodnotes wild: "I'm willing to tell you; I'm wanting to tell you; I'm waiting to tell you." That's the Welsh strain in him. (*To* DOOLITTLE) How did you know Eliza was here if you didn't send her?

DOOLITTLE: She sent back for her luggage, and I got to hear about it. She said she didn't want no clothes. What was I to think from that, Governor. I ask you as a parient, what was I to think?

HIGGINS: So you came to rescue her from worse than death, eh?

DOOLITTLE (*relieved at being so well understood*): Just so, Governor. That's right.

HIGGINS: Mrs. Pearce, Eliza's father has come to take her away. Give her to him.

DOOLITTLE (*desperately*): Now wait a minute, Governor, wait a minute. You and me is men of the world, ain't we?

HIGGINS: Oh! Men of the world, are we? You'd better go, Mrs. Pearce.

MRS. PEARCE: I think so indeed, sir! (*She goes with dignity.*)

DOOLITTLE: Governor, I've taken a sort of fancy to you. (*Again he wheezes in* HIGGINS' *face, causing the latter almost to lose balance.*) And if you want the girl I'm not so set on havin' her back home again, but what I might be open to is an arrangement. All I ask is my rights as a father; and you're the last man alive to expect me to let her go for nothing; for I can see you're one of the straight sort, Governor. Well, what's a five-pound note to you? And what's Eliza to me?

PICKERING: I think you ought to know, Doolittle, that Mr. Higgins' intentions are entirely honorable.

DOOLITTLE (*to* PICKERING): Of course they are, Governor. If I thought they wasn't, I'd ask fifty.

HIGGINS (*revolted*): Do you mean to say that you would sell your daughter for fifty pounds?

PICKERING: Have you no morals, man?

DOOLITTLE (*frankly*): No! I can't afford 'em, Governor. Neither could you if you was as poor as me. Not that I mean any harm, mind ya . . . but . . . if Eliza is going to get a bit out of this, why not me, too? Eh? Look at it my way. What am I? I ask ya, what am I? I'm one of the undeserving poor, that's what I am. Think what that means to a man. It means he's up agenst middle-class morality for all the time. If there's anything going and I put in for a bit of it, it's always the same story: you're undeserving, so you can't have it. But my needs is as great as the most deserving widow's that ever got money out of six different charities in one week for the death of the same husband. I don't need less than a deserving man, I need more. I don't eat less hearty than he does, and I drink a lot more. I'm playing straight with you. I ain't pretending to be deserving. I'm undeserving, and I mean to go on being undeserving. I like it, and that's the truth. But will you take advantage of a man's nature to do him out of the price of his own daughter what he's brought up, fed and clothed by the sweat of his brow, till she's growed big enough to be interesting to you two gentlemen? Is five pounds unreasonable? I put it to you, and I leave it to you.

HIGGINS: You know, Pickering, if we were to take this man in hand for three months, he could choose between a seat in the Cabinet and a popular pulpit in Wales. I suppose we ought to give him a fiver?

PICKERING: He'll make bad use of it, I'm afraid.

DOOLITTLE: Not me, so help me, Governor, I won't. Just one good spree for myself and the missus, givin' pleasure to ourselves and employment to others, and satisfaction to you to know it ain't been throwed away. You couldn't spend it better.

HIGGINS: This is irresistible. Let's give him ten. (*He goes to his desk for his wallet.*)

DOOLITTLE: No! The missus wouldn't have the heart to spend ten, Governor; ten pounds is a lot of money: it makes a man feel prudent-like; and then goodbye to happiness. No, you give me what I ask for, Governor: not a penny less, not a penny more.

PICKERING: I rather draw the line at encouraging this sort of immorality. Doolittle, why don't you marry that missus of yours? After all, marriage is not so frightening. You married Eliza's mother?

DOOLITTLE: Who told you that, Governor?

PICKERING (*stunned*): Well, nobody told me. But I concluded naturally . . .

(DOOLITTLE *emphatically shakes his head to the contrary.*)

HIGGINS (*returning with a five-pound note*): Pickering, if we listen to this man another minute we shall have no convictions left. Five pounds, I think you said?

DOOLITTLE (*taking it*): Thank you, Governor.

(*He hurries for the door, anxious to get away with his booty. In the rush, he collides with a rather nicely dressed, clean, but angry young woman with a copy book in her hand. It is, of course,* ELIZA, *whom he does not recognize.* MRS. PEARCE *is with her.*)

ELIZA (*in a rage*): I won't! I won't! I won't!

DOOLITTLE (*at the collision*): Beg pardon, miss!

ELIZA (*ignoring him and confronting* HIGGINS): I won't say those ruddy vowels one more time!

DOOLITTLE: Blimey, it's Eliza! I never thought she'd clean up so good-lookin'. She does me credit, don't she, Governor?

ELIZA (*her anger heightened by his presence*): Here! What are you doin' here?

DOOLITTLE (*sternly*): You hold your tongue and don't you give these gentlemen none of your lip. If you have any trouble with her, Governor, give her a few licks of the strap. That's the way to improve her mind. (*He bows low.*) Good mornin', gentlemen. (*Cheerfully whacking* ELIZA *on the backside*) Cheerio, Eliza. (*He goes out the door in such high good spirits he cannot resist laughing out loud.*)

HIGGINS: By George, there's a man for you! A philosophical genius of the first water. Mrs. Pearce, write to Mr. Ezra Wallingford and tell him if he wants a lecturer to get in touch with Mr. Alfred P. Doolittle, a common dustman—but one of the most original moralists in England.

MRS. PEARCE: Yes, sir. (*She goes.*)

ELIZA: Here, what did he come for?

HIGGINS: Say your vowels.

ELIZA (*ready to explode at the mention of them*): I know my vowels. I knew them before I came.

HIGGINS: If you know them, say them.

ELIZA: Ahyee, E, Iyee, Ow, You!

HIGGINS (*thundering*): Stop! Say: A. E. I. O. U!

ELIZA: That's what I said: Ahyee, E, Iyee, Ow, You. I've been syin' them for three days, and I won't sy them no more!

PICKERING (*gently*): I know it's difficult, Miss Doolittle. But try to understand . . .

HIGGINS: No use explaining, Pickering. As a military man you ought to know that. Drilling is what she needs. Much better leave her or she'll be turning to you for sympathy.

PICKERING: All right, if you insist, but have a little patience with her, Higgins. (*He goes out the door.*)

HIGGINS: Of course. (*To* ELIZA) Say "A."

ELIZA: You ain't go no heart, you ain't.

HIGGINS: "A."

ELIZA: Ahyee!

HIGGINS (*walks up the stairs saying "A" with each step,* ELIZA *defiantly echoing "Ahyee." When he reaches the landing he addresses her with firm resolve*): Eliza, I promise you you will pronounce your vowels correctly before this day is out, or there'll be no lunch, no dinner, and no chocolates! (*He exits through the door on the landing, punctuating his threat with a slam of the door.*)

(ELIZA, *in a blind rage, slams her study book down on the floor and stamps on it.*)

ELIZA:

> Just you wait, 'enry 'iggins, just you wait!
> You'll be sorry but your tears'll be too late!

You'll be broke and I'll have money;
Will I help you? Don't be funny!
Just you wait, 'enry 'iggins, just you wait!

Just you wait, 'enry 'iggins, till you're sick,
And you scream to fetch a doctor double-quick.
I'll be off a second later
And go straight to the the-ater!
Oh ho ho, 'enry 'iggins, just you wait!

Ooooooooh 'enry 'iggins!
Just you wait until we're swimmin' in the sea!
Ooooooooh 'enry 'iggins!
And you get a cramp a little ways from me!

When you yell you're going to drown
I'll get dressed and go to town!
Oh ho ho, 'enry 'iggins!
Oh ho ho, 'enry 'iggins!
Just you wait!

One day I'll be famous! I'll be proper and prim;
Go to St. James so often I will call it St. Jim!
One evening the King will say: "Oh, Liza, old thing,
I want all of England your praises to sing.
Next week on the twentieth of May
I proclaim Liza Doolittle Day!
All the people will celebrate the glory of you,
And whatever you wish and want I gladly will do."

"Thanks a lot, King," says I, in a manner well-bred;
"But all I want is 'enry 'iggins' 'ead!"
"Done," says the King, with a stroke.
"Guard, run and bring in the bloke!"

Then they'll march you, 'enry 'iggins, to the wall;
And the King will tell me: "Liza, sound the call."
As they raise their rifles higher,
I'll shout: "Ready! Aim! Fire!"

Oh ho ho! 'enry 'iggins!
Down you'll go! *'enry 'iggins!*
Just you wait!!!

Blackout

(*The lights come up in the study.* ELIZA *is on the stool in front of the desk.* HIGGINS *is in the alcove repairing a metronome.* PICKERING *as usual is in the wing chair reading the London* Times.)

ELIZA: The rine in spine sties minely in the pline.

HIGGINS (*correcting her*): The rain in Spain stays mainly in the plain.

ELIZA: Didn't I sy that?

HIGGINS: No, Eliza, you didn't "sy" that. You didn't even "say" that. (*He picks up a small burner and brings it down to the desk.*) Every night before you get into bed, where you used to say your prayers, I want you to repeat: "The rain in Spain stays mainly in the plain," fifty times. You will get much further with the Lord if you learn not to offend His ears. Now for your "H's." Pickering, this is going to be ghastly!

PICKERING: Control yourself, Higgins. Give the girl a chance.

HIGGINS (*patiently*): Of course. No one expects her to get it right the first time. Watch closely, Eliza. (*He places the burner on the desk and lights the flame.*) You see this flame? Every time you say your aitch properly, the flame will waver. Every time you drop your aitch, the flame will remain stationary. That's how you will know you've done it correctly; in time your ear will hear the difference. Now, listen carefully; in Hertford, Hereford and Hampshire, hurricanes hardly ever happen.

(ELIZA *sits down behind the desk.*)
Now repeat after me, In Hertford, Hereford and Hampshire, hurricanes hardly ever happen.

ELIZA (*conscientiously*): In 'ertford, 'ereford and 'ampshire, 'urricanes 'ahdly hever 'appen!

HIGGINS (*infuriated*): No, no, no, no! Have you no ear at all?

ELIZA (*willingly*): Should I do it over?

HIGGINS: No. Please, no! We must start from the very beginning. (*He kneels before the flame.*) Do this: ha, ha, ha, ha. (*He rises.*)

ELIZA: Ha—ha—ha—ha. (*She looks up at him happily.*)

HIGGINS: Well, go on. Go on.

(ELIZA *continues.* HIGGINS *strolls casually over to* PICK- ERING, *leaving* ELIZA *to aspirate at the flame.*)

Does the same thing hold true in India, Pickering; the peculiar habit of not only dropping a letter like the letter aitch, but using it where it shouldn't be? Like "hever" instead of "ever"? You'll notice some of the Slavic peoples when they learn to speak English have a tendency to that with their G's. They say "linger" (soft g) instead of "linger" (hard g); and then they turn around and say "singer" (hard g) instead of "singer" (soft g).

(PICKERING *had never thought about it and naturally is perplexed.*)

I wonder why that's so. I must look it up.

(HIGGINS *starts for the landing.* ELIZA, *by this time, is sinking fast from lack of oxygen.* PICKERING *notices her dying gasps and pulls* HIGGINS' *arm to call his attention to it.*)

(*Thinking which book to consult*)

Go on! Go on!

(*He continues up the stairs.* ELIZA *musters together one final "HA" and blows out the flame. The room is plunged into darkness.*)

(*In the darkness, six* SERVANTS *emerge, and stand in a spotlight at the far end of the study.*)

SERVANTS:

> Poor Professor Higgins!
> Poor Professor Higgins!
> Night and day
> He slaves away!
> Oh, poor Professor Higgins!
> All day long
> On his feet;

Up and down until he's numb;
Doesn't rest;
Doesn't eat;
Doesn't touch a crumb!

(*The spotlight goes off. The* SERVANTS *disappear and the lights come up in the study.* PICKERING *is seated in his favorite chair with a large and fulsome tea table before him.* ELIZA *is on the sofa.* HIGGINS *is standing by the xylophone, a cup in one hand, a xylophone mallet in the other. He taps out eight notes. "How kind of you to let me come.")*

HIGGINS: *Kind* of you, *kind* of you, *kind* of you. Now listen, Eliza. (*He plays them again.*) How kind of you to let me come.

ELIZA: How kind of *you* to let me come.

HIGGINS (*puts down the mallet in despair and walks over to the tea table*): No! *Kind* of you. It's just like "*cup* of tea." *Kind* of you—*cup* of tea. *Kind* of you—Say "cup of tea."

ELIZA (*hungrily*): Cappatea.

HIGGINS: No! No! A cup of tea . . . (*Takes a mouthful of cake from the tray*) It's awfully good cake. I wonder where Mrs. Pearce gets it?

PICKERING: Mmmmm! First rate! The strawberry tarts are delicious. And did you try the pline cake?

(HIGGINS *looks at him in horror and then turns to* ELIZA.)

HIGGINS: Now, try it again, Eliza. A cup of tea. A cup of tea.

ELIZA (*longingly*): A cappatea.

HIGGINS: Can't you hear the difference? Put your tongue forward until it squeezes against the top of your lower teeth. Now say "cup."

ELIZA (*her attention only on the cake in* HIGGINS' *hand*): C-cup.

HIGGINS: Now say "of."

ELIZA: Of.

HIGGINS: Now say, cup, cup, cup, cup—of, of, of, of.

ELIZA: Cup, cup, cup, cup—of, of, of, of! Cup, cup, cup, cup—of, of, of, of . . .

PICKERING (*as she's practicing*): By Jove, that was a glorious tea, Higgins. Do finish the strawberry tart. I couldn't eat another thing.

HIGGINS: No, thanks, old chap, really.

PICKERING: It's a shame to waste it.

HIGGINS: Oh, it won't go to waste. (*He takes the last tart.*) I know someone who's immensely fond of strawberry tarts.

(ELIZA'S *eyes light up hopefully. But alas,* HIGGINS *walks right past her and goes to the bird cage.*)

HIGGINS (*pushing the cake through the bars*): *Cheep, cheep, cheep!*

ELIZA (*shrieking*): Aaaaaaaaaaaooooooooowwww!!

            Blackout

(*The lights black out and the* SERVANTS *again appear in the spotlight.*)

SERVANTS:

    Poor Professor Higgins!
    Poor Professor Higgins!
    On he plods
    Against all odds;
    Oh, poor Professor Higgins!
    Nine P.M.
    Ten P.M.
    On through midnight ev'ry night.
    One A.M.
    Two A.M.
    Three . . . !

(*The spotlight goes off. The* SERVANTS *disappear and the lights come up again in the study.* ELIZA *is seated in the wing chair.* HIGGINS *has drawn up the stool and is facing her, a small box of marbles in his hand. He is placing them in her mouth.*)

HIGGINS: Four . . . five . . . six marbles. There we are. (*He holds up a slip of paper.*) Now, I want you to read this and enunciate each word just as if the marbles were not in your mouth. "With blackest moss, the flower pots were thickly crusted, one and all." Each word clear as a bell. (*He gives her the paper.*)

ELIZA (*unintelligibly*): With blackest moss the flower pots . . . I can't! I can't!

PICKERING (*from the sofa*): I say, Higgins, are those pebbles really necessary?

HIGGINS: If they were necessary for Demosthenes, they are necessary for Eliza Doolittle. Go on, Eliza.

ELIZA (*trying again with no better results*): With blackest moss, the flower pots were thickly crusted, one and all. . . .

HIGGINS: I cannot understand a word. Not a word.

ELIZA (*her anger coming through the marbles and "flower pots"*): With blackest moss, the flower pots were thickly crusted, one and all; the rusted nails fell from the knots that held the pear to the gable-wall . . .

PICKERING (*soon after she has begun*): I say, Higgins, perhaps the poem is too difficult for the girl. Why don't you try a simpler one, like: "The Owl and the Pussycat"? Oh, yes, that's a charming one.

HIGGINS (*bellowing*): Pickering! I cannot hear the girl!

(ELIZA *gasps and takes the marbles out of her mouth.*) What's the matter? Why did you stop?

ELIZA: I swallowed one.

HIGGINS (*reassuringly*): Oh, don't worry. I have plenty more. Open your mouth.

(*The lights go out and into the spotlight again appear the* SERVANTS.)

SERVANTS:

> Quit, Professor Higgins!
> Quit, Professor Higgins!
> Hear our plea
> Or payday we
> Will quit, Professor Higgins!
> Ay not I,
> O not Ow,

Pounding, pounding in our brain.
Ay not I,
O, not Ow,
Don't say "Rine," say "Rain" . . .

(*The spotlight goes off. The* SERVANTS *disappear and the lights come up again on the study.* ELIZA *is draped wearily on the sofa.* PICKERING *is half asleep in the wing chair.* HIGGINS *is seated at his desk, an ice-bag on his head. The gray light outside the windows indicates the early hours of the morning.*)

HIGGINS (*wearily*): The rain in Spain stays mainly in the plain.

ELIZA: I can't. I'm so tired. I'm so tired.

PICKERING (*half asleep*): Oh, for heaven's sake, Higgins. It must be three o'clock in the morning. Do be reasonable.

HIGGINS (*rising*): I am always reasonable. Eliza, if I can go on with a blistering headache, you can.

ELIZA: I have a headache, too.

HIGGINS: Here.

(*He plops the ice-bag on her head. She takes it off her head and buries her face in her hands, exhausted to the point of tears.*)

(*With sudden gentleness*) Eliza, I know you're tired. I know your head aches. I know your nerves are as raw as meat in a butcher's window. But think what you're trying to accomplish. (*He sits next to her on sofa.*) Think what you're dealing with. The majesty and grandeur of the English language. It's the greatest possession we have. The noblest sentiments that ever flowed in the hearts of men are contained in its extraordinary, imaginative and musical mixtures of sounds. That's what you've set yourself to conquer, Eliza. And conquer it you will. (*He rises, goes to the chair behind his desk and seats himself heavily.*) Now, try it again.

ELIZA (*slowly*): The rain in Spain stays mainly in the plain.

HIGGINS (*sitting up*): What was that?

ELIZA: The rain in Spain stays mainly in the plain.
HIGGINS (*rising, unbelievably*): Again.
ELIZA: The rain in Spain stays mainly in the plain.
HIGGINS (*to* PICKERING): I think she's got it! I think she's got it!
ELIZA: The rain in Spain stays mainly in the plain.
HIGGINS (*triumphantly*):

By George, she's got it!
By George, she's got it!

Now once again, where does it rain?
ELIZA: On the plain! On the plain!
HIGGINS: And where's that soggy plain?
ELIZA: In Spain! In Spain!
(PICKERING *jumps to his feet and the three sing out joyously.*)
THE THREE:

The rain in Spain stays mainly in the plain!
The rain in Spain stays mainly in the plain!

(HIGGINS *walks excitedly to the xylophone.*)
HIGGINS: In Hertford, Hereford and Hampshire . . . ?
ELIZA: Hurricanes hardly happen.
(*Higgins taps out "How kind of you to let me come."*)
ELIZA: How kind of you to let me come!
HIGGINS (*putting down the mallet and turning back to her*): Now once again, where does it rain?
ELIZA: On the plain! On the plain!
HIGGINS: And where's that blasted plain?
ELIZA: In Spain! In Spain!

THE THREE:

The rain in Spain stays mainly in the plain!
The rain in Spain stays mainly in the plain!

(*Joy and victory!* HIGGINS *takes a handkerchief from*

his pocket and waves it in front of PICKERING *who charges it like the finest bull in Spain.* HIGGINS *turns and grabs* ELIZA *and they do a few awkward tango steps while* PICKERING *jumps around like a flamenco dancer shouting "Viva Higgins, Viva."* HIGGINS *swings* ELIZA *onto the sofa and joins* PICKERING *in a bit of heel-clicking.* ELIZA *jumps down from the sofa. They throw themselves into a wild jig and then all collapse back upon the sofa engulfed in laughter.*)

(MRS. PEARCE *enters in her nightrobe, followed by two of the* SERVANTS *who have also been awakened.*)

HIGGINS: Pickering, we're making fine progress. I think the time has come to try her out.

MRS. PEARCE (*making her presence known*): Are you feeling all right, Mr. Higgins?

HIGGINS: Quite well, thank you, Mrs. Pearce. And you?

MRS. PEARCE: Very well, sir, thank you.

HIGGINS: Splendid. (*To* PICKERING) Let's test her in public and see how she fares.

MRS. PEARCE: Mr. Higgins, I was awakened by a dreadful pounding. Do you know what it might have been?

HIGGINS: Pounding? I heard no pounding. Did you, Pickering?

PICKERING (*innocently*): No.

HIGGINS: If this continues, Mrs. Pearce, I should see a doctor. Pickering, I know! Let's take her to the races.

PICKERING (*rising*): The races!?

HIGGINS (*rising too, excited by the idea*): Yes! My mother's box at Ascot.

PICKERING (*cautiously*): You'll consult your mother first, of course.

HIGGINS: Of course. (*Thinking better of it*) No! We'll surprise her. Let's go straight to bed. First thing in the morning we'll go off and buy her a dress. Eliza, go on with your work.

MRS. PEARCE: But, Mr. Higgins, it's early in the morning!

HIGGINS: What better time to work than early in the

morning? (*To* PICKERING) Where does one buy a lady's gown?

PICKERING: Whiteley's, of course.

HIGGINS: How do you know that?

PICKERING: Common knowledge.

HIGGINS (*studying* PICKERING *carefully*): We mustn't get her anything too flowery. I despise those gowns with a sort of weed here and a weed there. Something simple, modest and elegant is what's called for. Perhaps with a sash. (*He places the imaginary sash on* PICKERING'S *hip and steps back to eye it.*) Yes. Just right.

(*He goes out the door.* PICKERING *looks down at his hip to reassure himself the sash is not there and follows after him.*)

(MRS. PEARCE, *whose face has been a study in amazement, goes quickly to* ELIZA.)

MRS. PEARCE: You've all been working much too hard. I think the strain is beginning to show. Eliza, I don't care what Mr. Higgins says, you must put down your books and go to bed.

ELIZA (*lost on an errant cloud only hears her from far below*):

> Bed! Bed! I couldn't go to bed!
> My head's too light to try to set it down!
> Sleep! Sleep! I couldn't sleep tonight!
> Not for all the jewels in the crown!
>
> I could have danced all night!
> I could have danced all night!
> And still have begged for more.
> I could have spread my wings
> And done a thousand things
> I've never done before.
>
> I'll never know
> What made it so exciting,
> Why all at once
> My heart took flight.

I only know when he
Began to dance with me,
I could have danced, danced, danced all night!

1ST SERVANT (*to* ELIZA): It's after three, now.
2ND SERVANT (*to* MRS. PEARCE):

Don't you agree, now,
She ought to be in bed?

(MRS. PEARCE *nods emphatically.*)
ELIZA (*telling the* SERVANTS):

I could have danced all night!
I could have danced all night!
And still have begged for more.
I could have spread my wings
And done a thousand things
I've never done before.

SERVANTS (*simultaneously telling* ELIZA):

You're tired out.
You must be dead.
Your face is drawn.
Your eyes are red.
Now say goodnight, please.
Turn out the light, please.
It's really time
For you to be in bed.
Do come along.
Do as you're told,
Or Mrs. Pearce
Is apt to scold.
You're up too late, miss.
And sure as fate, miss.
You'll catch a cold.

(MRS. PEARCE *goes to the alcove for a comforter.*)

ELIZA:

> I'll never know
> What made it so exciting,
> Why all at once
> My heart took flight.
> I only know when he
> Began to dance with me
> I could have danced, danced, danced all night!

SERVANTS (*simultaneously*):

> Put down your book
> The work'll keep.
> Now settle down
> And go to sleep.

(ELIZA *stretches out on the sofa and* MRS. PEARCE *covers her with a comforter.*)

MRS. PEARCE:

> I understand, dear.
> It's all been grand, dear.
> But now it's time to sleep.

(*She turns out the lights and she and the* SERVANTS *go.*)

ELIZA (*reliving it*):

> I could have danced all night!
> I could have danced all night!
> And still have begged for more.
> I could have spread my wings
> And done a thousand things
> I've never done before.
> I'll never know
> What made it so exciting,
> Why all at once
> My heart took flight.

(*She throws off the comforter and jumps to her feet.*)

> I only know when he
> Began to dance with me
> I could have danced, danced, danced all night!

Scene 6

Near the race meeting, Ascot.

Time: A sunny July afternoon.

At Rise: PICKERING, *dressed for Ascot, is strolling toward the club tent with* MRS. HIGGINS. MRS. HIGGINS, *elegantly gowned, is a woman a shade perhaps beyond sixty.* CHARLES, MRS. HIGGINS' *chauffeur, follows dutifully behind.* MRS. HIGGINS, *obviously perplexed by* PICKERING'S *conversation, pauses.*

MRS. HIGGINS: Colonel Pickering, I don't understand. Do you mean that my son is coming to Ascot today?

PICKERING: Yes, he is, Mrs. Higgins. As a matter of fact, he's here!

MRS. HIGGINS (*dismayed*): What a disagreeable surprise. Ascot is usually the one place I can come to with my friends and not run the risk of seeing my son, Henry. Whenever my friends meet him, I never see them again.

PICKERING: He had to come, Mrs. Higgins. You see, he's taking the girl to the annual Embassy Ball, and he wanted to try her out first.

MRS. HIGGINS (*blank bewilderment*): I beg your pardon?

PICKERING (*clearing it up*): You know, the annual Embassy Ball.

MRS. HIGGINS: Yes, I know the ball; but what girl?

PICKERING: Oh, didn't I mention that?

MRS. HIGGINS: No, you did not.

PICKERING: Well, it's quite simple, really. One night I

went to the Opera at Covent Garden to hear one of my favorite operas, *Aida;* and as I was coming out— incidentally, they didn't do *Aida* that night. No, they did *Götterdämmerung* instead. I'd never heard *Götterdämmerung.* By George, that's a rackety one! When the tenor chap . . .

MRS. HIGGINS (*impatiently*): What about the girl, Colonel?

PICKERING: Oh, yes. As I was coming out, I met your son, Henry, who, in turn, met Miss Doolittle, who now lives with Henry.

MRS. HIGGINS: Lives with Henry? (*Hopefully*) Is it a love affair?

PICKERING: Heavens no! She's a flower girl. He picked her up off the kerbstone.

MRS. HIGGINS (*not quite believing her ears*): A flower girl?

PICKERING: Yes. Higgins said to me: "Pickering, you see this girl? In six months I could make a duchess of her." I said: "Nonsense." He came right back with: "Yes, I can." "All right," I said, "I'll make a bet with you you can't." And I did. And he is.

MRS. HIGGINS: But, Colonel, I still don't understand.

(*A distant bell is heard ringing.*)

CHARLES: The horses are leaving the paddock, Mrs. Higgins.

PICKERING: Excuse me, Mrs. Higgins. I must fetch her. (*He tips his hat politely and moves and starts off.*)

MRS. HIGGINS: But, Colonel, am I to understand that Henry is bringing a flower girl to Ascot?

PICKERING (*turning, delighted that* MRS. HIGGINS *finally understands*): Yes, Mrs. Higgins! That's it, that's it precisely! Jolly good, Mrs. Higgins! Jolly good!

MRS. HIGGINS (*calmly*): Charles, you'd better stay close to the car. I may be leaving abruptly. (*She sweeps off.*)

Scene 7

Inside a club tent, Ascot.

There is an archway in the center and two large pouffes on either side. To view the races one would look out at the mythical "fourth wall."

Time: Immediately following.

At Rise: The stage is filled with ladies and gentlemen of Ascot all appropriately attired for the occasion. At this precise moment, they are standing in groups looking out at the race track, the immobility of their faces and bodies registering their abiding disdain from any emotional display.

LADIES AND GENTLEMEN:

Ev'ry duke and earl and peer is here.
Ev'ry one who should be here is here.
What a smashing, positively dashing
Spectacle: the Ascot op'ning day.

At the gate are all the horses
Waiting for the cue to fly away.
What a gripping, absolutely ripping
Moment at the Ascot op'ning day.

Pulses rushing!
Faces flushing!
Heartbeats speed up!
I have never been so keyed up!

Any second now
They'll begin to run.
Hark! a bell is ringing,
They are springing
Forward
Look! It has begun . . . !

(*In stony silence and with a reserve indistinguishable from boredom they observe the progress of the race.*)

What a frenzied moment that was!
Didn't they maintain an exhausting pace?
'Twas a thrilling, absolutely chilling
Running of the Ascot op'ning race.

(*To the strains of this Gavotte they move cautiously about, finally disappearing.* MRS. HIGGINS *enters and bows graciously to one or two as they go off. Almost immediately* HIGGINS *enters briskly, dressed in tweeds.*)

HIGGINS (*to himself*): I don't know where the devil they could be. (*He sees his mother and comes to her.*) Oh, darling, have you seen Pickering? My, you do look nice! (*Kisses her*)

MRS. HIGGINS: I saw Colonel Pickering, and Henry, dear, I'm most provoked. I've heard you've brought a common flower girl from Covent Garden to my box at Ascot.

HIGGINS: Oh, darling, she'll be all right. I've taught her to speak properly, and she has strict orders as to her behavior. She's to keep to two subjects: the weather and everybody's health—sort of "fine day" and "how do you do," and not just let herself go on things in general. Help her along, darling, and you'll be quite safe.

MRS. HIGGINS: Safe? To talk about our health in the middle of a race?

HIGGINS (*impatiently*): Well, she's got to talk about something. (*His eyes wander about in search of them.*)

MRS. HIGGINS: Henry, you're not even dressed properly.

HIGGINS: I changed my shirt.

MRS. HIGGINS: Where is the girl now?

HIGGINS: Being pinned. Some of the clothes we bought for her didn't quite fit. I told Pickering we should have taken her with us.

MRS. HIGGINS: You're a pretty pair of babies playing with your live doll.

(MRS. EYNSFORD-HILL, FREDDY EYNSFORD-HILL *and*

LORD *and* LADY BOXINGTON, *an elderly couple, stroll on.* MRS. HIGGINS *greets them.*)
Ah, Mrs. Eynsford-Hill!

HIGGINS: Oh damn, are all these people with you? (*He walks away.*)

MRS. EYNSFORD-HILL: Mrs. Higgins, is this your celebrated son?

MRS. HIGGINS: I'm sorry to say my celebrated son has no manners. He may be the life and soul of the Royal Society soirées, but he's rather trying on more commonplace occasions.

(PICKERING *enters followed by* ELIZA, *who is exquisitely dressed; she produces an impression of remarkable distinction and beauty.*)

HIGGINS (*seeing them*): Ah!

MRS. HIGGINS: Ah, Colonel Pickering, you're just in time for tea.

PICKERING: Thank you. Mrs. Higgins, may I introduce Miss Eliza Doolittle?

MRS. HIGGINS (*extending her hand graciously*): My dear Miss Doolittle.

ELIZA (*speaking with pedantic correctness of pronunciation and great beauty of tone*): How kind of you to let me come. (*She says it properly and* HIGGINS *nods his approval.*)

MRS. HIGGINS: Delighted, my dear. (*Introducing*) Mrs. Eynsford-Hill. Miss Doolittle.

MRS. EYNSFORD-HILL: How do you do?

ELIZA: How do you do? (*She gasps slightly in making sure of the H in "how" but is quite successful.*)

MRS. HIGGINS (*introducing*): Lord and Lady Boxington. Miss Doolittle.

LORD AND LADY BOXINGTON: How do you do?

ELIZA: How do you do?

MRS. HIGGINS (*introducing*): And Freddy Eynsford-Hill.

ELIZA: How do you do?

FREDDY (*instantly infatuated*): How do you do?

HIGGINS: Miss Doolittle?

ELIZA: Good afternoon, Professor Higgins.

(HIGGINS *motions for her to sit down, she looks at him blankly. He pantomimes sitting down and she does. They all seat themselves on the two pouffes,* ELIZA *finding herself between* MRS. HIGGINS *and* FREDDY. HIGGINS, *of course, stays on his feet.* TWO STEWARDS *serve tea.*)

FREDDY: The first race was very exciting, Miss Doolittle. I'm so sorry you missed it.

MRS. HIGGINS (*hurriedly*): Will it rain do you think?

ELIZA: The rain in Spain stays mainly in the plain.

(HIGGINS *irresistibly does a quick fandango step which is so bizarre that the others have nothing to do but pretend it didn't happen.*)

But in Hertford, Hereford and Hampshire hurricanes hardly ever happen.

FREDDY: Ha ha, how awfully funny.

ELIZA: What is wrong with that, young man? I bet I got it right.

FREDDY: Smashing!

MRS. EYNSFORD-HILL: I do hope we won't have any unseasonably cold spells. It brings on so much influenza, and our whole family is susceptible to it.

ELIZA (*darkly*): My aunt died of influenza, so they said. (MRS. EYNSFORD-HILL *clicks her tongue sympathetically.*) But it's my belief they done the old woman in.

(HIGGINS *and* PICKERING *look at each other accusingly as if each blames the other for having taught* ELIZA *this last unrehearsed phrase.*)

MRS. HIGGINS (*puzzled*): Done her in?

ELIZA: Yes, Lord love you! Why should she die of influenza when she come through diphtheria right enough the year before? Fairly blue with it she was. They all thought she was dead; but my father, he kept ladling gin down her throat.

(HIGGINS, *for want of something to do, balances his tea cup on his head and takes several steps without spilling it. Quite a feat.*)

Then she came to so sudden that she bit the bowl off the spoon.

MRS. HIGGINS (*startled*): Dear me!

ELIZA (*piling up the indictment*): Now, what call would a woman with that strength in her have to die of influenza, and what become of her new straw hat that should have come to me? Somebody pinched it.

(HIGGINS *fans himself with a silver tray off the tea cart.*) And what I say is, them as pinched it, done her in.

LORD BOXINGTON (*nervously loud*): Done her in? Done her in, did you say?

HIGGINS (*hastily*): Oh, that's the new small talk. To do a person in means to kill them.

MRS. EYNSFORD-HILL (*to* ELIZA, *horrified*): You surely don't believe your aunt was killed?

ELIZA: Do I not! Them she lived with would have killed her for a hatpin, let alone a hat.

MRS. EYNSFORD-HILL: But it can't have been right for your father to pour spirits down her throat like that. It might have killed her.

ELIZA: Not her. Gin was mother's milk to her.

(PICKERING *stiffens.* HIGGINS *decides to leave, tips his hat to all, and starts off. However, his uncontrollable curiosity holds him at the last moment to hear what else* ELIZA *has to say.*)

Besides, he'd poured so much down his own throat that he knew the good of it.

LORD BOXINGTON: Do you mean that he drank?

ELIZA: Drank! My word! Something chronic. (*To* FREDDY, *who is in convulsions of suppressed laughter*) Here! What are you sniggering at?

FREDDY: The new small talk. You do it so awfully well.

ELIZA: If I was doing it proper, what was you laughing at? (*To* HIGGINS) Have I said anything I oughtn't?

MRS. HIGGINS (*interposing*): Not at all, my dear.

ELIZA: Well, that's a mercy, anyhow. (*Expansively*) What I always say is . . .

(PICKERING *jumps to his feet. He and* HIGGINS *make a number of desperate signals and strange sounds to prevent her from going on.*)

PICKERING (*rushing to* ELIZA): I don't suppose there's

enough time before the next race to place a bet? (*To* ELIZA) Come, my dear.

(ELIZA *rises.*)

MRS. HIGGINS: I'm afraid not, Colonel Pickering.

(*They all rise as several of the ladies and gentlemen enter to take their positions for the next race.*)

FREDDY: I have a bet on number seven. I should be so happy if you would take it. You'll enjoy the race ever so much more. (*He offers her a race ticket. She accepts.*)

ELIZA: That's very kind of you.

(FREDDY *leads* ELIZA *to a vantage point directly center.*)

FREDDY: His name is Dover.

ELIZA (*repeating the name*): Dover.

LADIES *and* GENTLEMEN *and* ALL (*except* HIGGINS):

> There they are again
> Lining up to run.
> Now they're holding steady,
> They are ready
> For it.
> Look! It has begun!

(*Again the mummified silence. The one exception is* ELIZA. *Clenching her fists with excitement, she leans forward. Oblivious to the deportment of those around her, she begins to cheer her horse on.*)

ELIZA (*at first softly*): Come on, come on, Dover!

(*The* LADIES *and* GENTLEMEN *slowly turn to stare at her and look at each other in wonder.*)

Come on, come on, Dover!

(*Her voice crescendoes. The* LADIES *and* GENTLEMEN *move perceptibly away from this ugly exhibition of natural behavior.*)

Come on, Dover!!! Move your bloomin' arse!!!

(*An agonizing moan rises up from the crowd. The moment she says it she realizes what she has done and brings her hand to her mouth as if trying to push the words back in. Several women gracefully faint, and are caught by their escorts.* LORD *and* LADY BOXINGTON *are staggered.* PICKERING *flies from the scene running faster than Dover.* HIGGINS, *of course, roars with laughter.*)

Scene 8

Outside HIGGINS' *house, Wimpole Street.*

Time: Later that day.

At Rise: A CONSTABLE *is strolling along the street.* FREDDY, *a man with a purpose, walks up to the* CONSTABLE.

FREDDY: Officer, I know this is Wimpole Street, but could you tell me where 27-A is?

POLICEMAN (*indicating* HIGGINS' *house*): Right there, sir.

FREDDY: Thank you. (*The* CONSTABLE *strolls on.* FREDDY *starts for the door when a* FLOWER GIRL *passes, looking very much as* ELIZA *used to, carrying a basket of flowers.* FREDDY *stops her.*) Are those for sale?

FLOWER GIRL: Yes, sir. A shilling.

(FREDDY *takes a shilling from his pocket—his last— and gives it to the* FLOWER GIRL *in exchange for a small nosegay.*)

FREDDY: Here.

FLOWER GIRL: Thank you kindly, sir.

FREDDY (*with radiant good spirits*): Isn't it a heavenly day?

(*The* FLOWER GIRL *looks up at the sky which is quite overcast. Thinking him undoubtedly mad, she hurries on.*)

(FREDDY *knocks on* HIGGINS' *door and while awaiting response, irrepressibly gives vent to his feelings.*)

FREDDY:

> When she mentioned how her aunt bit off the spoon,
> She completely done me in.
> And my heart went on a journey to the moon,

When she told about her father and the gin.
And I never saw a more enchanting farce,
Than the moment when she shouted "move your
    bloomin' " . . .

MRS. PEARCE (*opens the door*): Yes, sir?
FREDDY: Is Miss Doolittle at home?
MRS. PEARCE: Who shall I say is calling?
FREDDY: Freddy Eynsford-Hill. If she doesn't remem-
ber me, tell her I'm the chap who was sniggering at her.
MRS. PEARCE (*looking at him strangely*): Yes, sir.
FREDDY: And would you give her these? (*Hands her
the nosegay*)
MRS. PEARCE: Yes, sir. (*She takes them and moves quickly
to get the door between her and this odd young man.*)
FREDDY: You needn't rush. (*Gazing lovingly down the
street*) I want to drink in this street where she lives.
MRS. PEARCE: Yes, sir. (*She goes into the house.*)
FREDDY:

I have often walked down this street before;
But the pavement always stayed beneath my feet before.
All at once am I
Several stories high.
Knowing I'm on the street where you live.

Are there lilac trees in the heart of town?
Can you hear a lark in any other part of town?
Does enchantment pour
Out of ev'ry door?
No, it's just on the street where you live!

And oh! the towering feeling
Just to know somehow you are near!
The overpowering feeling
That any second you may suddenly appear!

People stop and stare. They don't bother me.
For there's nowhere else on earth that I would rather be.

Let the time go by,
I won't care if I
Can be here on the street where you live.

(MRS. PEARCE *opens the door.*)

MRS. PEARCE (*cautiously*): Mr. Eynsford-Hill?

FREDDY: Yes?

MRS. PEARCE: I'm terribly sorry, sir. Miss Doolittle says she doesn't want to see anyone ever again.

FREDDY: But why? She was magnificent!

MRS. PEARCE: Magnificent? (*Not believing her ears*) Do you have the right address, sir?

FREDDY (*with calm resolution*): Of course. Tell her I'll wait.

MRS. PEARCE: But it might be days, sir. Even weeks!

FREDDY: But don't you see? I'll be happier here.

(MRS. PEARCE *hastily goes back into the house.*)

FREDDY:

People stop and stare. They don't bother me.
For there's nowhere else on earth that I would rather be.
Let the time go by,
I won't care if I
Can be here on the street where you live.

(FREDDY *settles himself down on the doorstep for the long wait.*)

Scene 9

HIGGINS' *study. There is a decanter of port and two glasses on the desk, next to them a carnation.*

Time: Evening. Six weeks later.

At Rise: HIGGINS, *in white tie, is pacing slowly up and down the room, thoughtfully detached.* PICKERING, *also formally dressed, is obviously nervous.*

PICKERING: Higgins, if there's any mishap at the Embassy tonight, if Miss Doolittle suffers any embarrassment whatever, it's on your head alone. I've been begging you to call off this experiment ever since Ascot.

HIGGINS (*calmly*): Eliza can do anything. (*He continues his stroll.*)

PICKERING: But suppose she's discovered? Suppose she makes another ghastly mistake?

HIGGINS (*good-humoredly*): There'll be no horses at the ball, Pickering.

PICKERING (*in a panic*): But think how agonizing it would be! If anything happened tonight, I don't know what I'd do.

HIGGINS (*helpfully*): You could always rejoin your regiment.

PICKERING (*exploding*): Higgins, this is no time for flippancy. The way you've driven her these last six weeks has exceeded all the bounds of common . . . Higgins, stop pacing up and down! Can't you settle someplace?

HIGGINS: Have some port. It will quieten your nerves.

PICKERING: I'm not nervous! Where is it?

HIGGINS: On the desk.

(PICKERING *goes to it and helps himself to a glass.*)
(MRS. PEARCE *comes out of the door on the landing.*)

MRS. PEARCE: The car is here, sir.

HIGGINS: Thank you, Mrs. Pearce. Are you helping Eliza?

MRS. PEARCE: Yes, sir. (*She goes.*)

PICKERING: Help her, indeed! I'll bet the gown doesn't fit. I warned you about those French designers. You should have gone to a good English store, where you knew everybody was on our side. Have a little port.

HIGGINS: No, thank you.

PICKERING: It will quieten your nerves.

HIGGINS (*still pacing*): No, thank you.

PICKERING (*exasperated*): Are you so sure she'll retain all you've hammered into her?

HIGGINS: We shall see.

PICKERING: But suppose she doesn't?

HIGGINS: Then I lose my bet. (*He settles himself comfortably on the sofa.*)

PICKERING (*slightly irritated*): You know what I can't stand about you, Higgins? It's your confounded complacency. In a moment like this, with so much at stake, it's utterly indecent that you don't need a little port. What of the girl? You act as if she doesn't matter at all.

HIGGINS: Rubbish, Pickering. Of course she matters. What do you think I've been doing all these months? What could possibly matter more than to take a human being and change her into a different human being by creating a new speech for her? Why, it's filling up the deepest gulf that separates class from class, and soul from soul. She matters immensely.

(ELIZA *appears on the landing—a vision. She walks down the stairs and into the room.* HIGGINS *rises.* PICKERING *is overcome by her appearance.* HIGGINS *circles her inspecting her carefully.*)

PICKERING: Miss Doolittle, you look beautiful.

ELIZA: Thank you, Colonel Pickering.

PICKERING: Don't you think so, Higgins?

(ELIZA *turns to* HIGGINS *hopefully.*)

HIGGINS (*having decided the gown is quite all right*): Not bad. Not bad at all.

(*The* BUTLER *and* FOOTMAN *enter with coats, hats and* ELIZA's *cape and help each into his.* HIGGINS *goes to the desk for his carnation which he slips into his buttonhole, then looking furtively around to make certain* PICKERING *doesn't see him, he pours himself a quick glass of port. He starts briskly for the door. At the threshold, he pauses, turns and gazes at* ELIZA. *He returns to her and offers his arm. She takes it and they go out the door,* PICKERING *following after.*)

Scene 10

The Promenade outside the ballroom of the Embassy.

Time: Late that evening.

At Rise: A FOOTMAN *is on the landing announcing the guests as the names are given to him from a* FOOTMAN *above. The Promenade is filled with couples, some strolling on, some engaged in conversation with others.* MRS. HIGGINS *is chatting with friends.*

FOOTMAN: Sir Reginald and Lady Tarrington.

(SIR REGINALD *and* LADY TARRINGTON *descend the stairs and join friends in the room.*)

FOOTMAN: Professor Zoltan Karpathy.

(KARPATHY *comes into the room. He is an important-looking man with an astonishingly hairy face. He has an enormous mustache flowing out into luxuriant whiskers. His hair glows with oil. He is wearing several worthless orders. Obviously a foreigner, one would guess him as Hungarian in which case one would be right. In spite of the ferocity of his mustache, he is amiable and genially voluble. He joins some friends.*)

FOOTMAN: Colonel Hugh Pickering.

(PICKERING *enters looking about for* MRS. HIGGINS. *Seeing her, he goes to her.*)

PICKERING: Mrs. Higgins!

MRS. HIGGINS (*to her group*): Excuse me. (*She and* PICKERING *separate themselves.*)

PICKERING: Well, she got by the first hurdle. (*With muffled excitement*) The Ambassador's wife was completely captivated.

MRS. HIGGINS: I know. I've heard several people asking who she is. Do tell me what happened.

PICKERING: Higgins said: "Madame Ambassador, may I introduce Miss Eliza Doolittle?" and Madame Ambassador said: "How do you do?" And Eliza came right back with: "How do you do?"

MRS. HIGGINS (*disappointed*): Is that all?

PICKERING: Oh, no! When it was my turn, both the Ambassador and his wife said to me: "Colonel Pickering, who is that captivating creature with Professor Higgins?"

MRS. HIGGINS: What did you say?

PICKERING: Well, I was stopped for a moment. Then I collected myself and I said: "Eliza Doolittle."

MRS. HIGGINS (*with sardonic appreciation*): That was very quick thinking, Colonel.

PICKERING (*puffing up*): Thank you. Mrs. Higgins, do you think Eliza will make it?

MRS. HIGGINS: Oh, I hope so! I've grown terribly fond of that girl.

FOOTMAN: Professor Henry Higgins.

(HIGGINS *appears on landing.* KARPATHY, *hearing his name, turns. As* HIGGINS *descends into the room,* KARPATHY *flings his arms wide apart and approaches him enthusiastically.*)

KARPATHY: Ah, maestro! Maestro! (*He kisses* HIGGINS *on both cheeks.*)

HIGGINS (*surprised, annoyed and wounded by the whiskers*): Oh! Oh!

KARPATHY: You remember me?

HIGGINS: No, I don't. Who the devil are you?

KARPATHY: I am your pupil, your first, best and greatest pupil. I am Zoltan Karpathy, that marvelous boy. I have made your name famous throughout Europe. You teach me phonetics. You cannot forget me.

HIGGINS: Why don't you shave?

KARPATHY: I have not your imposing appearance; your figure, your brow. Nobody notice me when I shave.

HIGGINS (*noticing his chest full of medals*): Where did you find all those old coins?

KARPATHY (*not at all offended—he can't be*): Decorations for language. The Queen of Transylvania is here this evening. I am indispensable to her at these international parties. I speak thirty-two languages. I know everybody in Europe. No imposter escape my detection. And now, Professor, you must introduce me to this glorious creature you escort this evening. She fascinate everyone. Not since Mrs. Langtry came to London . . .

FOOTMAN: His Excellency Dr. Themistocles Stephanos.

(*A well-decorated gentleman and his lady descend the stairs and join a group.*)

KARPATHY (*lowering his voice*): This so-called Greek diplomat pretends he cannot speak English. But he does not deceive me. He is the son of a Yorkshire watchmaker. He speaks English so villainously that he dare not utter a word of it without betraying his origin. I help him to pretend, but I make him pay through the nose. I make them all pay. (*He irritatingly strokes* HIGGINS' *lapel.*) I look forward to meeting your lady. (*He bows, a bit too low, and rejoins his group.*)

(PICKERING, *who has overheard this conversation, is in a state when* HIGGINS *goes to him.*)

PICKERING: Higgins, I say!

MRS. HIGGINS (*nervously*): Where's Eliza?

HIGGINS: Upstairs. Last minute adjustment.

PICKERING: I say, Higgins, let's not risk it. Let's collect her and leave immediately.

MRS. HIGGINS: Henry, do you think it wise to stay?

HIGGINS: Stay? Why not?

FOOTMAN: Miss Eliza Doolittle.

(ELIZA *descends the stairs.* HIGGINS *crosses to join her at the foot. Everyone turns and everyone stares.* KARPA-THY *immediately comes forward.*)

KARPATHY: Ah, Professor, you must introduce me . . .

(*He is interrupted by the strains of a regal march as the* QUEEN OF TRANSYLVANIA *and* CONSORT *make their grand entrance into the room. He retreats and joins in the mass bowing. As the* QUEEN *passes* ELIZA *she is caught by her loveliness and places her hand lightly on her cheek.*)

QUEEN: Charming. Charming.

(*The* QUEEN *and* CONSORT *proceed to the ballroom as everyone rises to follow.*)

Scene 11

The Ballroom of the Embassy. Sumptuous. Decorous.

Time: Immediately following.

Everyone has followed the QUEEN *into the ballroom. The waltz begins.* PROFESSOR KARPATHY *comes forward again and bows to* HIGGINS, *inviting an introduction.* HIG-

GINS *bows cheerfully in return, takes* ELIZA *in his arms and dances away with her.*

KARPATHY, *now suspicious indeed, walks away. Slowly, the ballroom fills with couples whirling about in three-quarter time.* ELIZA *and* HIGGINS *dance off. Everyone changes partners and* ELIZA *returns in the arms of another.* KARPATHY *dances his partner closer and closer to her. When partners are changed again,* ELIZA *finds herself dancing with* KARPATHY. *Inaudibly because of the music,* KARPATHY *leads her into animated conversation; so animated in fact, they stop dancing as the others continue waltzing around them.*

PICKERING *enters and sees them. He frantically waves across the room to attract* HIGGINS' *attention.* HIGGINS *comes forward.* PICKERING, *by gestures, entreats* HIGGINS *to interrupt* KARPATHY *and* ELIZA; *but* HIGGINS, *regarding this as the ultimate test, decides to do nothing but watch and see what will happen.*

The curtain descends slowly.

ACT TWO

Scene 1

HIGGINS' *study.*

Time: 3:00 the following morning.

At Rise: The SERVANTS, *having tried to stay awake to learn the outcome of the ball, have lost their battle with sleep, and are in various positions of oblivion in the room. The clock strikes 3.* MRS. PEARCE *enters to awaken them as the sounds of voices are heard in the outside hall. They jump to their feet as* HIGGINS *and* PICKERING *enter.*

ELIZA *follows. She is tired. Her expression is almost tragic. Seemingly unnoticed by all, she walks to the corner of the room and stands motionless by the desk as the two* FOOTMEN *help* PICKERING *and* HIGGINS *off with their cloaks.*

PICKERING (*jubilant*): Higgins, it was an immense achievement.

HIGGINS (*yawning*): A silly notion. If I hadn't backed myself to do it, I should have chucked the whole thing up two months ago.

PICKERING: Absolutely fantastic.

HIGGINS: A lot of tomfoolery.

PICKERING: Higgins, I salute you.

HIGGINS: Nonsense, the silly people don't know their own silly business.

183

PICKERING:

> Tonight, old man, you did it!
> You did it! You did it!
> You said that you would do it,
> And indeed you did.
> I thought that you would rue it;
> I doubted you'd do it.
> But now I must admit it
> That succeed you did.
> You should get a medal
> Or be even made a knight.

HIGGINS: It was nothing. Really nothing.

PICKERING:

> All alone you hurdled
> Ev'ry obstacle in sight.

HIGGINS:

> Now, wait! Now, wait!
> Give credit where it's due.
> A lot of the glory goes to you.

(ELIZA *flinches violently but they take no notice of her. She recovers herself and stands stonily as before.*)

PICKERING:

> But you're the one who did it,
> Who did it, who did it!
> As sturdy as Gibraltar,
> Not a second did you falter.
> There's no doubt about it,
> You did it!

> (*To* MRS. PEARCE)

> I must have aged a year tonight.
> At times I thought I'd die of fright.
> Never was there a momentary lull.

HIGGINS (*lighting a cigar*):

> Shortly after we came in
> I saw at once we'd eas'ly win;
> And after that I found it deadly dull.

PICKERING (*to* MRS. PEARCE *and* MAIDS):

> You should have heard the ooh's and ah's;
> Ev'ry one wond'ring who she was.

HIGGINS: You'd think they'd never seen a lady before.
PICKERING:

> And when the Prince of Transylvania
> Asked to meet her,
> And gave his arm to lead her to the floor . . . !

> (*To* HIGGINS)

> I said to him: You did it!
> You did it! You did it!
> They thought she was ecstatic
> And so damned aristocratic,
> And they never knew
> That you
> Did it!

(ELIZA's *beauty becomes murderous.*)
HIGGINS: Thank Heavens for Zoltan Karpathy. If it weren't for him I would have died of boredom. He was there, all right. And up to his old tricks.
MRS. PEARCE: Karpathy? That dreadful Hungarian? Was he there?
HIGGINS: Yes.
(*The* SERVANTS *gather around him, hanging on every word.*)
(*In his best dramatic manner*)

That blackguard who uses the science of speech
More to blackmail and swindle than teach;
He made it the devilish business of his
"To find out who this Miss Doolittle is."

Ev'ry time we looked around
There he was, that hairy hound
From Budapest.
Never leaving us alone,
Never have I ever known
A ruder pest.
Fin'lly I decided it was foolish
Not to let him have his chance with her.
So I stepped aside and let him dance with her.

Oozing charm from ev'ry pore,
He oiled his way around the floor.
Ev'ry trick that he could play,
He used to strip her mask away.
And when at last the dance was done
He glowed as if he knew he'd won!
And with a voice too eager,
And a smile too broad,
He announced to the hostess
That she was a fraud!

MRS. PEARCE: No!
HIGGINS: Yavol!

Her English is too good, he said,
Which clearly indicates that she is foreign.
Whereas others are instructed in their native language
English people aren.
And although she may have studied with an expert
Di'lectician and grammarian,
I can tell that she was born Hungarian!

(*He and* PICKERING *roar with laughter.*)

Not only Hungarian, but of royal blood, she is a princess!

(*The* SERVANTS *can no longer contain their admiration.*)

SERVANTS:

> Congratulations, Professor Higgins,
> For your glorious victory!
> Congratulations, Professor Higgins!
> You'll be mentioned in history!

(HIGGINS *accepts this spontaneous demonstration graciously. He seats himself on the sofa and modestly puffs his cigar.*)

FOOTMAN: THE REST OF THE SERVANTS:

This evening, sir, you did it!   Congratulations,
You did it! You did it!   Professor Higgins!
You said that you would do it! For your glorious
And indeed you did.   Victory!

This evening, sir, you did it!   Congratulations,
You did it! You did it!   Professor Higgins!
We know that we have said it, Sing a hail and halleluia
But—you did it and the credit Ev'ry bit of credit
For it all belongs to you!   For it all belongs to you!

(PICKERING *joins in this final musical bravo.*)

HIGGINS (*rising*): All I can say is, thank God it's all over. Now I can go to bed at last without dreading tomorrow.

(*The* SERVANTS *go off to bed.*)

MRS. PEARCE: Goodnight, Mr. Higgins. (*She, too, goes.*)

HIGGINS: Goodnight.

PICKERING: I think I shall turn in, too. It's been a great occasion. Goodnight, Higgins. (*He goes.*)

HIGGINS: Goodnight, Pickering. Oh, Mrs. Pearce! (*But*

she is gone.) Oh damn, I meant to tell her I wanted coffee in the morning instead of tea. Leave a little note for her, Eliza, will you? (*He looks around the room.*) What the devil have I done with my slippers?

(*The slippers are by the desk.* ELIZA *tries to control herself, but no longer can. She hurls them at him with all her force.*)

ELIZA: There are your slippers! And there! Take your slippers, and may you never have a day's luck with them!

HIGGINS (*astounded*): What on earth? (*He comes to her.*) What's the matter? Is anything wrong?

ELIZA (*seething*): Nothing wrong—with you. I've won your bet for you, haven't I? That's enough for you. I don't matter, I suppose?

HIGGINS: You won my bet! You! Presumptuous insect. *I* won it! What did you throw those slippers at me for?

ELIZA: Because I wanted to smash your face. I'd like to kill you, you selfish brute. Why didn't you leave me where you picked me out of—in the gutter? You thank God it's all over, and that now you can throw me back again there, do you?

HIGGINS (*looking at her in cool wonder*): So the creature is nervous, after all?

(ELIZA *gives a suffocated scream of fury and instinctively darts her nails in his face.* HIGGINS *catches her wrists.*)

Ah! Claws in you, you cat! How dare you show your temper to me? (*He throws her roughly onto the sofa.*) Sit down and be quiet.

ELIZA (*crushed by superior strength and weight*): What's to become of me? What's to become of me?

HIGGINS: How the devil do I know what's to become of you? What does it matter what becomes of you?

ELIZA: You don't care. I know you don't care. You wouldn't care if I was dead. I'm nothing to you—not so much as them slippers.

HIGGINS (*thundering*): *Those* slippers.

ELIZA (*with bitter submission*): Those slippers. I didn't think it made any difference now.

(*A pause.* ELIZA *hopeless and crushed,* HIGGINS *a little uneasy.*)

HIGGINS (*in his loftiest manner*): Why have you suddenly begun going on like this? May I ask whether you complain of your treatment here?

ELIZA: No.

HIGGINS: Has anybody behaved badly to you? Colonel Pickering? Mrs. Pearce?

ELIZA: No.

HIGGINS: You don't pretend that I have treated you badly?

ELIZA: No.

HIGGINS: I'm glad to hear it. (*He moderates his tone.*) Perhaps you're tired after the strain of the day? (*He picks up a box of chocolates.*) Have a chocolate?

ELIZA: No. (*Recollecting her manners*) Thank you.

HIGGINS (*good-humored again*): I suppose it was natural for you to be anxious, but it's all over now. (*He pats her kindly on the shoulder. She writhes.*) There's nothing more to worry about.

ELIZA: No, nothing more for you to worry about. Oh God, I wish I was dead.

HIGGINS (*in sincere surprise*): Why, in Heaven's name, why? Listen to me, Eliza. All this irritation is purely subjective.

ELIZA: I don't understand. I'm too ignorant.

HIGGINS: It's only imagination. Nobody's hurting you. Nothing's wrong. You go to bed like a good girl, and sleep it off. Have a little cry and say your prayers; that will make you comfortable.

ELIZA: I heard your prayers. "Thank God it's all over!"

HIGGINS (*impatiently*): Well, don't you thank God it's all over? Now you are free and can do what you like.

ELIZA (*pulling herself together in desperation*): What am I fit for? What have you left me fit for? Where am I to go? What am I to do? What's to become of me?

HIGGINS (*enlightened, but not at all impressed*): Oh, that's what's worrying you, is it? (*Condescending to a trivial subject out of pure kindness*) Oh, I shouldn't bother about that if I were you. I should imagine you won't have much difficulty in settling yourself somewhere or other—though I hadn't quite realized you were going away. You might marry, you know. You see, Eliza, all men are not confirmed old bachelors like me and the Colonel. Most men are the marrying sort, poor devils. And you're not bad-looking. It's quite a pleasure to look at you at times. (*He looks at her.*) Not now, of course. You've been crying and look like the very devil; but when you're all right and quite yourself, you're what I should call attractive. Come, you go to bed and have a good night's rest; and then get up and look at yourself in the glass; and you won't feel so cheap. (*Peering into the box of chocolates, in search of a creamy one. In the process, a genial afterthought occurs to him.*) I daresay my mother could find some chap or other who would do very well.

ELIZA: We were above that in Covent Garden.

HIGGINS: What do you mean?

ELIZA: I sold flowers. I didn't sell myself. Now you've made a lady of me, I'm not fit to sell anything else.

HIGGINS: Tosh, Eliza, don't insult human relations by dragging all that cant about buying and selling into it. (*Not finding a creamy one, he puts the chocolates down.*) You needn't marry the fellow if you don't want to.

ELIZA: What else am I to do?

HIGGINS: Oh, lots of things. What about that old idea of a florist's shop? Pickering could set you up in one. He's lots of money. (*Chuckling*) He'll have to pay for all those togs you've been wearing; and that, with the hire of the jewelry, will make a big hole in two hundred pounds. Oh, come! You'll be all right. I must clear off to bed; I'm devilish sleepy. By the way, I was looking for something. What was it?

ELIZA: Your slippers.

HIGGINS: Yes, of course. You shied them at me.

(*He picks them up and is starting for the stairs when she rises and speaks to him.*)

ELIZA: Before you go, sir—

HIGGINS (*stopping, surprised at her calling him "sir"*): Eh?

ELIZA: Do my clothes belong to me or to Colonel Pickering?

HIGGINS (*coming back to her as if her question were the very climax of unreason*): What the devil use would they be to Pickering? Why need you start bothering about that in the middle of the night?

ELIZA: I want to know what I may take away with me. I don't want to be accused of stealing.

HIGGINS (*deeply wounded*): Stealing? You shouldn't have said that, Eliza. That shows a want of feeling.

ELIZA: I'm sorry. I'm only a common, ignorant girl; and in my station, I have to be careful. There can't be any feelings between the like of you and the like of me. Please will you tell me what belongs to me and what doesn't?

HIGGINS (*very sulky*): You may take the whole damned houseful if you like. Except the jewels. They're hired. Will that satisfy you? (*He turns on his heels and is about to go in extreme dudgeon.*)

ELIZA (*drinking in his emotion like nectar and nagging him to provoke a further supply*): Stop, please! (*She takes off jewels.*) Will you take these to your room and keep them safe? I don't want to run the risk of their being missing.

HIGGINS (*furious*): Hand them over!

(*She gives him the jewels, he crams them into his pocket, unconsciously decorating himself with the protruding ends of the chains.*)
If these belonged to me instead of the jeweler, I'd ram them down your ungrateful throat.

ELIZA (*taking a ring off*): This ring isn't the jeweler's; it's the one you bought me in Brighton. I don't want it now. (*He throws the ring violently across the room and turns on her so threateningly that she crouches with her hands over her face, and exclaims*) Don't you hit me.

HIGGINS: Hit you! You infamous creature, how dare you accuse me of such a thing? It is you who have hit me. You have wounded me to the heart.

ELIZA (*thrilling with hidden joy*): I'm glad. I've got a little of my own back, anyhow.

HIGGINS (*with dignity, in his finest professional style*): You have caused me to lose my temper, a thing that has hardly ever happened to me before. I prefer to say nothing more tonight. I am going to bed. (*He starts up the stairs.*)

ELIZA (*pertly*): You'd better leave your own note for Mrs. Pearce about the coffee, for it won't be done by me!

HIGGINS (*stopping about halfway up the stairs*): Damn Mrs. Pearce! And damn the coffee! And damn you! And damn my own folly in having lavished my hard-earned knowledge and the treasure of my regard and intimacy on a heartless guttersnipe!

(*He marches up the stairs with impressive decorum and spoils it by tripping on the top step. He successfully recovers but while looking to see if she noticed his awkwardness, he runs into the table and inadvertently turns on the machine. Guttural vowel sounds come pouring through the speaker. He turns it off violently and with a slam of the door, disappears.*) (ELIZA *runs to the ring on the floor and picks it up.*)

ELIZA (*with smoldering fury*):

Just you wait, Henry Higgins, just you wait!
You'll be sorry but your tears'll be too late!
You will be the one it's done to;
And you'll have no one to run to;
Just you wait, Henry Higgins, just you . . .

(*She gives way to uncontrollable sobs.*)

Scene 2

Outside HIGGINS' *house.*

Time: Immediately following.

At Rise: FREDDY, *who has only left his post for changes of clothing, food and sleep, is seated on the doorstep.*
FREDDY (*undaunted*):

Are there lilac trees in the heart of town?
Can you hear a lark in any other part of town?
Does enchantment pour
Out of ev'ry door?
No, it's just on the street where you live!

And oh! the towering feeling
Just to know somehow she is near!
The overpowering feeling
That any second you may suddenly appear!

(ELIZA *comes out of the house. She is wearing a day-time suit and is carrying a small suitcase. For the moment,* FREDDY *doesn't see her.*)

People stop and stare. They don't . . .

(*He sees her now.*)
Darling!
ELIZA (*in a rage he does not understand*): What are you doing here?
FREDDY: Nothing. I spend most of my time here. Oh, don't laugh at me, Miss Doolittle, but this is the only place . . .
ELIZA (*she puts down suitcase and grabs him by the shoulders*): Freddy, you don't think I'm a heartless guttersnipe, do you?
FREDDY: Oh, no, darling. How could you imagine such a thing? You know how I feel. I've written you two and three times a day telling you. Sheets and sheets . . .

Speak and the world is full of singing,
And I'm winging
Higher than the birds.

(*In disgust, she turns away.*)

Touch and my heart begins to crumble,
The heavens tumble,
Darling, and I'm . . .

ELIZA (*turning on him violently*):

Words!
Words! Words! I'm so sick of words!
I get words all day through;
First from him, now from you!
Is that all you blighters can do?

(FREDDY *is frightened.*)

Don't talk of stars
Burning above;
If you're in love,
Show me!

Tell me no dreams
Filled with desire.
If you're on fire,
Show me!

(*He opens his arms to show her and she pushes him away.*)

Here we are together in the middle of the night!
Don't talk of spring! Just hold me tight!
Anyone who's ever been in love'll tell you that
This is no time for a chat!

Haven't your lips
Longed for my touch?
Don't say how much,
Show me! Show me!

Don't talk of love lasting through time.
Make me no undying vow.
Show me now!

(*Bewildered but happy, he reaches for her again. She grabs his arm and fairly flings him down the street.*)

Sing me no song!
Read me no rhyme!
Don't waste my time,
Show me!

Don't talk of June!
Don't talk of fall!
Don't talk at all!
Show me!

Never do I ever want to hear another word.
There isn't one I haven't heard.
Here we are together in what ought to be a dream;
Say one more word and I'll scream!

Haven't your arms
Hungered for mine?
Please don't "expl'ine,"
Show me! Show me!

Don't wait until wrinkles and lines
Pop out all over my brow,
Show me now!

(*She picks up her suitcase and answers the longing look in his eyes by crowning him with it. Having released some of her anger against mankind in general, she marches off. He follows her, his arms out.*)
FREDDY: Darling . . . Darling . . . !

Scene 3

Covent Garden. The Flower Market. A huge glass-
enclosed market center. There is a public house just
outside.

Time: 5:00 that morning.

At Rise: The market is coming to life. At first a few,
then more and more vendors and flower girls walk on
and prepare for business. A few COSTERMONGERS *warm*
themselves around the smudge-pot fire. In the group are
four who were warming themselves the night HIGGINS *first*
met ELIZA. *One of them starts whistling a few bars of the*
tune they sang. Three others pick it up.

MEN AT THE FIRE:

> With one enormous chair . . .
> Oh, wouldn't it be loverly?
>
> Lots of choc'late for me to eat;
> Lots of coal makin' lots of heat;
> Warm face, warm hands, warm feet . . .
> Oh, wouldn't it be loverly?

(ELIZA *walks into view and gazes around. She sees two*
flower girls she used to know and goes over to them. They
jump to their feet as if they recognize her, then feel they've
made a mistake and walk quickly away, one of them re-
marking that this "swell" looks very much like ELIZA
DOOLITTLE.

(ELIZA *sees the men at the fire and hesitantly walks*
toward them.)

> Oh, so loverly sittin' absobloominlutely still!
> I would never budge till spring
> Crept over me winder sill.
> Someone's head restin' on my knee;
> Warm and tender as he can be,

Who takes good care of me.
Oh, wouldn't it be loverly . . . ?
Loverly! Loverly! . . .

(They become aware of her presence, and their voices trail off. One of them rises.)

THAT ONE: Good morning, miss. Can I help you?

ELIZA *(looking hopefully into his face)*: Do you mind if I warm my hands?

THAT ONE: Go right ahead, miss.

(She kneels down to warm her hands. They all stare at her uncomfortably. One of them leans forward as if he knows her.)

ELIZA: Yes?

MAN LEANING FORWARD *(now leaning back)*: Excuse me, miss. For a second there I thought you was somebody else.

ELIZA: Who?

SAME MAN: Forgive me, ma'am. Early morning light playing tricks with me eyes.

(He rises. They all do.)

1ST MAN: Can I get you a taxi, ma'am? A lady like you shouldn't be walkin' around London at this hour of the mornin'.

ELIZA *(sadly)*: No . . . thank you.

SAME MAN: Good morning, miss.

(They all move away from her, somewhat embarrassed. Two of them keep looking back, feeling that they know her from somewhere.)

ELIZA *(More alone than she has ever been, picks up a bunch of violets from a basket next to the fire and stares at it)*:

Someone's head resting on my knee;
Warm and tender as he can be,
Who takes good care of me;
Oh, wouldn't it be loverly . . .
Loverly! Loverly!
Loverly! Loverly!

(*She is interrupted by a loud commotion from the pub.* HARRY *enters. He is quite well-dressed. He is followed by the* BARTENDER.)

HARRY: Well, goodnight to you, Cecil. (*Calls into the pub*) Time to go, Alfie!

(DOOLITTLE *comes out of the pub. He is resplendently dressed as for a fashionable wedding and might be the bridegroom. A flower in his buttonhole, a dazzling silk hat and patent leather shoes complete the effect.*)

BARTENDER: Do come again, Mr. Doolittle. We value your patronage always.

DOOLITTLE (*grandly*): Thank you, my good man. (*He gives him a generous tip.*) Here, take the missus a trip to Brighton.

BARTENDER (*gratefully*): Thank you, Mr. Doolittle. (*He goes back into the pub.*)

ELIZA (*who has been watching, astounded*): Father!

DOOLITTLE (*seeing her*): You see, Harry, he has no mercy. Sent her down to spy on me in my misery, he did. Me own flesh and blood. (*He goes up to* ELIZA.) Well, I'm miserable, all right. You can tell him that straight.

ELIZA: What are you talking about? What are you dressed up for?

DOOLITTLE: As if you didn't know! Go on back to that Wimpole Street devil and tell him what he done to me.

ELIZA: What has he done to you?

DOOLITTLE: He's ruined me, that's all. Destroyed me happiness. Tied me up and delivered me into the hands of middle-class morality. And don't you defend him. Was it him or was it not him that wrote to an old American blighter named Wallingford that was giving five millions to found moral reform societies, and tell him the most original moralist in England was Mr. Alfred P. Doolittle, a common dustman?

ELIZA (*bitterly*): That sounds like one of his jokes.

DOOLITTLE: You may call it a joke. It put the lid on me, right enough! The bloke died and left me four thousand pounds a year in his bloomin' will.

JAMIE (*coming out of the pub*): Oh, come on, Alfie. In a couple of hours you have to be at the church.

(*A group of* DOOLITTLE's *friends also emerge and motion him to come on back.*)

ELIZA: Church?

DOOLITTLE (*tragically*): Yes, church. The deepest cut of all. Why do you think I'm dressed up like a ruddy pall-bearer? Your stepmother wants to marry me. Now I'm respectable—she wants to be respectable.

ELIZA: If that's the way you feel, why don't you give the money back?

DOOLITTLE (*with melancholy resignation*): That's the tragedy of it, Eliza. It's easy to say chuck it, but I haven't the nerve. We're all intimidated. Intimidated, Eliza, that's what we are. And that's what I am. Bought up. That's what your precious professor has brought me to.

ELIZA: Not my precious professor.

DOOLITTLE: Oh, sent you back, has he? First he shoves me in the middle-class, then he chucks you out for me to support you. All part of his plan. (*Resourcefully*) But you double-cross him. Don't you come home to me. Don't you take tuppence from me. You stand on your own two feet. You're a lady now and you can do it.

(FREDDY *appears through the crowd.*)

FREDDY: Eliza, it's getting awfully cold in that taxi.

DOOLITTLE: I say, you want to come and see me turned off this mornin'? St. George's, Hanover Square, ten o'clock. (*Sadly*) I wouldn't advise it, but you're welcome.

ELIZA: No, thank you, Dad.

FREDDY (*to* ELIZA): Are you all finished here?

ELIZA (*with great finality*): Yes, Freddy. I'm all finished here. (*She takes his arm.*) Good luck, Dad.

(*As a last gesture of farewell, she tosses away the violets and goes off with* FREDDY. DOOLITTLE *watches her go, rubbing his hands in satisfaction at having disposed of a knotty problem.*)

JAMIE: Come along, Alfie.

DOOLITTLE: How much time do I have left?

JAMIE, HARRY AND FRIENDS:

> There's just a few more hours.
> That's all the time you've got.
> A few more hours
> Before they tie the knot.

(DOOLITTLE *bows his head in despair.*)
DOOLITTLE: There are drinks and girls all over London, and I have to track 'em down in just a few more hours.

> I'm getting married in the morning!
> Ding dong! the bells are gonna chime.
> Pull out the stopper!
> Let's have a whopper!
> But get me to the church on time!

> I gotta be there in the mornin'
> Spruced up and lookin' in me prime.
> Girls, come and kiss me;
> Show how you'll miss me.
> But get me to the church on time!

> If I am dancin'
> Roll up the floor.
> If I am whistlin'
> Whewt me out the door!

> For I'm gettin' married in the mornin'
> Ding dong! the bells are gonna chime.
> Kick up a rumpus
> But don't lose the compass;
> And get me to the church,
> Get me to the church,
> For Gawd's sake, get me to the church on time!

DOOLITTLE AND EVERYONE:

> I'm getting married in the morning
> Ding dong! the bells are gonna chime.

DOOLITTLE:

Drug me or jail me,
Stamp me and mail me.

ALL:

But get me to the church on time!

I gotta be there in the morning
Spruced up and lookin' in me prime.

DOOLITTLE:

Some bloke who's able
Lift up the table.

ALL:

And get me to the church on time!

DOOLITTLE:

If I am flying
Then shoot me down.
If I am wooin',
Get her out of town!

ALL:

For I'm getting married in the morning!
Ding dong! the bells are gonna chime.

DOOLITTLE:

Feather and tar me;
Call out the Army;
But get me to the church.

ALL:

> Get me to the church . . .

DOOLITTLE: For Gawd's sake, get me to the church on time!!

(*The* CROWD *pulls out the stopper and has a whopper; a final street dance of farewell. When it's over, dawn begins to make her presence known through the glass roof.* DOO-LITTLE'S *friends line up to bid him a formal good-bye.*)

HARRY AND EVERYONE:

> Starlight is reelin' home to bed now.
> Mornin' is smearin' up the sky.
> London is wakin'.
> Daylight is breakin'.
> Good luck, old chum,
> Good health, good-bye.

DOOLITTLE (*solemnly shakes hands with all. In deepest gloom*):

> I'm gettin' married in the mornin'
> Ding dong! the bells are gonna chime . . .
> Hail and salute me
> Then haul off and boot me . . .
> And get me to the church,
> Get me to the church . . .
> For Gawd's sake, get me to the church on time!

(DOOLITTLE *is lifted high in the air and carried off to the grim inevitable.*)

Scene 4

The upstairs hall of HIGGINS' *house. There are three doors on the corridor and a telephone table and telephone.*

Time: Around 11:00, the following morning.

At Rise: HIGGINS *is bellowing from his room.*

HIGGINS: Pickering! Pickering!

(*He charges out of his room, followed by* MRS. PEARCE. *Having not finished dressing, he is wearing a dressing gown. He knocks violently on* PICKERING'S *door.*) Pickering! (*To* MRS. PEARCE) Didn't she say where to send her clothes?

MRS. PEARCE: I told you, sir, she took them all with her.

PICKERING (*entering; dressed*): What? What?

HIGGINS: Here's a confounded thing! Eliza's bolted!

PICKERING: Bolted?

HIGGINS: Yes, bolted! And Mrs. Pearce let her go without telling me a word about it.

PICKERING: Well, I'm dashed!

HIGGINS (*pacing distractedly up and down*): What am I to do? I got tea this morning instead of coffee. I can't find anything. I don't know what appointments I've got.

MRS. PEARCE: Eliza would know.

HIGGINS (*rage and frustration*): Of course she would, but damn it she's gone.

MRS. PEARCE: Did either of you gentlemen frighten her last night?

PICKERING: You were there, Mrs. Pearce. We hardly said a word to her. (*Turning on* HIGGINS) Higgins, did you bully her after I went to bed?

HIGGINS: Just the other way around. She threw the slippers at me. I never gave her the slightest provocation. The slippers came bang at my head before I uttered a word. And she used the most perfectly awful language. I was shocked.

PICKERING (*stunned*): Well, I'm dashed.

HIGGINS: I don't understand it. She was shown every possible consideration. She admitted it herself.

PICKERING (*stunned*): Well, I'm dashed.

HIGGINS (*wildly*): Pickering, stop being dashed and do something.

PICKERING: What?

HIGGINS: Call the police! What are they there for, in Heaven's name? (*He starts into his room.*)

MRS. PEARCE (*stopping him*): Mr. Higgins, you can't give Eliza's name to the police as if she were a thief, or a lost umbrella.

HIGGINS: Why not? I want to find her! The girl belongs to me! I paid five pounds for her! (*He charges into his room.*)

PICKERING: Quite right. (*He picks up phone.*) Scotland Yard, please. May I have some coffee, Mrs. Pearce?

MRS. PEARCE: Yes, sir. (*She goes.*)

PICKERING (*sunnily, into phone*): Oh, good morning, old chap. Colonel Hugh Pickering, here . . . 27-A Wimpole Street. I want to report a missing person. Anything you can do to assist in her recovery will be frightfully appreciated. I'm not without influence, and I'll see to it that your superiors . . . Oh, yes, Eliza Doolittle . . . about twenty-one . . . I should say about five foot seven . . . Her eyes?

HIGGINS (*yelling from his room*): Brown!

PICKERING (*into the phone*): Brown . . . Her hair? Well, it's a rather neutral, nondescript color. I should say more on the . . .

HIGGINS (*bounding from his room*): Brown! Brown! Brown! (*Bounding back into his room,*)

PICKERING (*into the phone*): Well, you heard what he said: brown . . . Yes, this is her residence . . . Between three and four in the morning . . . No . . . No . . . No . . . No relation at all. Let's just say a good friend. (*He laughs good-humoredly.*) Hmph? (*A troubled look clouds his face.*) Now, see here, my good man, I'm not at all pleased with the tenor of that question. What the girl does here is our affair. Your affair is to get her back so she can continue doing it! (*He hangs up furious with the inspector.* HIGGINS *comes out of his room. He is now almost dressed. Vexation knots his face.*)

HIGGINS:

What in all of Heaven could have prompted her to go?
After such a triumph at the ball?

What could have depressed her?
What could have possessed her?
I cannot understand the wretch at all!

(*Shaking his head in exasperation, he goes back into his room to finish dressing.*)

PICKERING (*who was only half listening, hits upon an idea. Calling to* HIGGINS): Higgins, I have an old school chum at the Home Office. Perhaps he can help. I'll call him. (*Picks up phone*) Whitehall seven, two, double four, please. (*He waits.*)

(HIGGINS *enters, struggling with his tie.*)

HIGGINS:

Women are irrational, that's all there is to that!
Their heads are full of cotton, hay, and rags!
They're nothing but exasperating, irritating,
Vacillating, calculating, agitating,
Maddening, and infuriating hags!

(*He returns to his room.*)

PICKERING (*into the phone*): Brewster Budgin, please . . . Yes, I'll wait! (*He waits.*)

(HIGGINS *enters.*)

HIGGINS: Pickering, why can't a woman be more like a man?

(PICKERING *looks at him, startled.*)

Yes. Why can't a woman be more like a man?
Men are so honest, so thoroughly square;
Eternally noble, historically fair;
Who when you win will always give your back a pat.
Why can't a woman be like that?
Why does ev'ryone do what the others do?
Can't a woman learn to use her head?
Why do they do everything their mothers do?
Why don't they grow up like their father instead?
Why can't a woman take after a man?
Men are so pleasant, so easy to please;

Whenever you're with them, you're always at ease.
Would you be slighted if I didn't speak for hours?

PICKERING: Of course not.
HIGGINS: Would you be livid if I had a drink or two?
PICKERING: Nonsense.
HIGGINS: Would you be wounded if I never sent you flowers?
PICKERING: Never.
HIGGINS:

Why can't a woman be like you?

One man in a million may shout a bit.
Now and then there's one with slight defects.
One perhaps whose truthfulness you doubt a bit
But by and large we are a marvelous sex!

Why can't a woman behave like a man?
Men are so friendly, good-natured and kind;
A better companion you never will find.
If I were hours late for dinner, would you bellow?

PICKERING: Of course not.
HIGGINS: If I forgot your silly birthday, would you fuss?
PICKERING: Nonsense.
HIGGINS: Would you complain if I took out another fellow?
PICKERING: Never.
HIGGINS: Why can't a woman be like us?
(*Livid that they're not, he goes back into his room slamming the door behind him.*)
PICKERING (*into phone*): Hello, is Brewster Budgin there, please? (*Pause*) Boozy! You'll never, never, never guess who this is! (*Disappointed*) . . . Yes, it is. By George, what a memory! How are you, old fellow? It's so good to hear your voice again . . . Thirty years? It is really? Yes . . . oceans of water . . . yes . . . Boozy, old chap, I'll tell you why I called. Something rather

unpleasant has happened at this end. Could I come right over and see you? Oh, good. I'll be right there. Thank you, Boozy. (*He hangs up as* MRS. PEARCE *enters with the coffee.*) I'm going over to the Home Office, Mrs. Pearce.

MRS. PEARCE: I do hope you find her, Colonel Pickering. Mr. Higgins will miss her.

PICKERING: Mr. Higgins will miss her! Blast Mr. Higgins! I'll miss her! (*He goes.*)

(MRS. PEARCE *places the coffee on the table as* HIGGINS *comes out of his room, now fully dressed.*)

HIGGINS: Pickering! Pickering! (*He looks around.*) Where's the Colonel?

MRS. PEARCE: He's gone to the Home Office, sir.

HIGGINS: Ah! You see, Mrs. Pearce? I'm disturbed and he runs to help. (*Touched*) Now there's a good fellow. Mrs. Pearce, you're a woman,

Why can't a woman be more like a man?
Men are so decent, such regular chaps.
Ready to help you through any mishaps.
Ready to buck you up whenever you are glum.
Why can't a woman be a chum?

Why is thinking something women never do?
Why is logic never even tried?
Straightening up their hair is all they ever do.
Why don't they straighten up the mess that's inside?

Why can't a woman be more like a man?
If I were a woman who'd been to a ball,
Been hailed as a princess by one and by all;
Would I start weeping like a bathtub overflowing?
And carry on as if my home were in a tree?
Would I run off and never tell me where I'm going?
Why can't a woman be like me?

(*He clamps his hat on his head and stalks off.*)

Scene 5

The conservatory of MRS. HIGGINS' *house.*

Time: Shortly after.

At Rise: MRS. HIGGINS *and* ELIZA *are having tea.*

MRS. HIGGINS: And you mean to say that after you did this wonderful thing for them without making a single mistake, they just sat there and never said a word to you? Never petted you, or admired you, or told you how splendid you'd been?

ELIZA: Not a word.

MRS. HIGGINS: That's simply appalling. I should not have thrown the slippers at him, I should have thrown the fire irons.

(ELIZA *smiles, but the smile is short-lived as* HIGGINS *is heard thundering from the entrance hall.*)

HIGGINS (*off*): Mother! Mother!

(ELIZA *looks fearful and rises to leave.*)

MRS. HIGGINS (*staying her*): I thought it wouldn't be long. Stay where you are, my dear.

HIGGINS (*off*): Mother, where the devil are you?

MRS. HIGGINS: Remember, last night you not only danced with a prince, but you behaved like a princess.

(ELIZA *collects herself as* HIGGINS *charges into the room.*)

HIGGINS: Mother, the damndest . . . ! (*He sees* ELIZA. *Amazed. Angry.*) You!

ELIZA (*giving a staggering exhibition of ease of manner*): How do you do, Professor Higgins? Are you quite well?

HIGGINS (*choking*): Am I . . . (*He can say no more.*)

ELIZA: But of course you are. You are never ill. Would you care for some tea?

HIGGINS: Don't you dare try that game on me! I taught it to you! Get up and come home and don't be a fool! You've caused me enough trouble for one morning!

MRS. HIGGINS: Very nicely put, indeed, Henry. No woman could resist such an invitation.

HIGGINS: How did this baggage get here in the first place?

MRS. HIGGINS: Eliza came to see me, and I was delighted to have her. And if you don't promise to behave yourself, I shall have to ask you to leave.

HIGGINS: You mean I'm to put on my Sunday manners for this thing I created out of the squashed cabbage leaves of Covent Garden?

MRS. HIGGINS (*calmly*): Yes, dear, that is precisely what I mean.

HIGGINS: I'll see her damned first! (*He walks to the rear of the conservatory and paces back and forth noisily.*)

MRS. HIGGINS (*to* ELIZA): How did you ever learn manners with my son around?

ELIZA (*sweetly, but making certain her voice carries*): It was very difficult. I should never have known how ladies and gentlemen behave if it hadn't been for Colonel Pickering. He always showed me that he felt and thought about me as if I were something better than a common flower girl. You see, Mrs. Higgins, apart from the things one can pick up, the difference between a lady and a flower girl is not how she behaves, but how she is treated. I shall always be a flower girl to Professor Higgins because he always treats me as a flower girl and always will. But I know that I shall always be a lady to Colonel Pickering because he always treats me as a lady, and always will.

(*There is a strange gnashing noise from the rear of the conservatory.*)

MRS. HIGGINS: Henry, please don't grind your teeth.

(*The* PARLOR MAID *enters.*)

MAID: The Vicar is here, madam. Shall I show him into the garden?

MRS. HIGGINS (*horrified*): The Vicar, and the Professor? Good Heavens, no! I'll see him in the library.

(*The* MAID *goes.* MRS. HIGGINS *rises to follow.*)

Eliza, if my son begins to break things, I give you full permission to have him evicted. (*At the door, she turns back to* HIGGINS.) Henry, dear, if I were you, I should stick to two subjects, the weather and your health. (*She goes.*)

(HIGGINS *comes down to the tea table. He looks at* ELIZA *quizzically; while deciding on a method of attack he pours himself some tea. He decides on restraint.*)

HIGGINS: Well, Eliza, you've had a bit of your own back, as you call it. Have you had enough? And are you going to be reasonable? Or do you want any more?

ELIZA: You want me back only to pick up your slippers and put up with your tempers and fetch and carry for you.

HIGGINS: I haven't said I wanted you back at all.

ELIZA (*turns to him*): Oh, indeed. Then what are we talking about?

HIGGINS: About you, not about me. If you come back I shall treat you just as I have always treated you. I can't change my nature; and I don't intend to change my manners. My manners are exactly the same as Colonel Pickering's.

ELIZA: That's not true. He treats a flower girl as if she was a duchess.

HIGGINS: And I treat a duchess as if she was a flower girl.

ELIZA: Oh, I see. (*She rises composedly and walks away.*) The same to everybody.

HIGGINS: Just so. (*He sits at the table.*) . . . The great secret, Eliza, is not having bad manners or good manners or any other particular sort of manners, but having the same manner for all human souls. The question is not whether I treat you rudely, but whether you ever heard me treat anyone else better.

ELIZA (*with sudden sincerity*): I don't care how you treat me. I don't mind your swearing at me. I shouldn't mind a black eye: I've had one before this. But I won't be passed over.

HIGGINS: Then get out of my way: for I won't stop for you. You talk about me as if I were a motor bus.

ELIZA: So you are a motor bus: all bounce and go, and no consideration for anyone. But I can get along without you. Don't think I can't.

HIGGINS: I know you can. I told you you could. (*Pause, seriously*) You never wondered, I suppose, whether I could get along without you.

ELIZA: Don't try to get around me. You'll have to.

HIGGINS (*arrogantly*): And so I can. Without you or any soul on earth. (*With sudden humility*) But I shall miss you, Eliza. I've learned something from your idiotic notions. I confess that humbly and gratefully.

ELIZA: Well, you have my voice on your gramophone. When you feel lonely without me you can turn it on. It's got no feelings to hurt.

HIGGINS: I can't turn your soul on.

ELIZA: Oh, you are a devil. You can twist the heart in a girl as easily as some can twist her arms to hurt her. What am I to come back for?

HIGGINS (*heartily*): For the fun of it. That's why I took you on.

ELIZA: And you may throw me out tomorrow if I don't do everything you want me to?

HIGGINS: Yes: and you may walk out tomorrow if I don't do everything you want me to.

ELIZA: And live with my father?

HIGGINS: Yes, or sell flowers. Or would you rather marry Pickering?

ELIZA (*fiercely*): I wouldn't marry you if you asked me; and you're nearer my age than what he is.

HIGGINS (*correcting her gently*): Than he is.

ELIZA (*losing her temper and walking away from him*): I'll talk as I like. You're not my teacher now. That's not what I want and don't you think it. I've always had chaps enough wanting me that way. Freddy Hill writes to me twice and three times a day, sheets and sheets.

HIGGINS (*coming to her*): Oh, in short, you want me to be as infatuated about you as he is. Is that it?

ELIZA (*facing him, much troubled*): No, I don't. That's not the sort of feeling I want from you. I want a little kindness. I know I'm a common ignorant girl, and you a book-learned gentleman; but I'm not dirt under your feet. What I done— (*Correcting herself*) What I did was not for the dresses and the taxis: I did it because we were pleasant together and I come—came to care for you; not to want you to make love to me, and not forgetting the difference between us, but more friendly like.

HIGGINS: Yes, of course. That's just how I feel. And how Pickering feels. Eliza, you're a fool.

ELIZA: That's not a proper answer to give me.

HIGGINS: It's all you'll get until you stop being a plain idiot. If you're going to be a lady you'll have to stop feeling neglected if the men you know don't spend half their time sniveling over you and the other half giving you black eyes. You find me cold, unfeeling, selfish, don't you? Very well: Be off with you to the sort of people you like. Marry some sentimental hog or other with lots of money, and a thick pair of lips to kiss you with and a thick pair of boots to kick you with. If you can't appreciate what you've got, you'd better get what you can appreciate.

ELIZA (*desperate*): I can't talk to you: you turn everything against me. I'm always in the wrong. But don't you be too sure that you have me under your feet to be trampled on and talked down. I'll marry Freddy, I will, as soon as I'm able to support him.

HIGGINS (*disagreeably surprised*): Freddy!! That poor devil who couldn't get a job as an errand boy even if he had the guts to try for it! Woman, do you not understand? I have made you a consort for a king!

ELIZA: Freddy loves me: that makes him king enough for me. I don't want him to work: he wasn't brought up to it as I was. (*Determinedly*) I'll go and be a teacher.

HIGGINS: What'll you teach, in heaven's name?

ELIZA: What you taught me. I'll teach phonetics.

HIGGINS: Ha! Ha! Ha!

ELIZA: I'll offer myself as an assistant to that brilliant Hungarian!

HIGGINS (*in a fury*): What! That imposter! That humbug!

That toadying ignoramus! Teach him my methods! My discoveries? (*He strides toward her.*) You take one step in that direction and I'll wring your neck. Do you hear?

ELIZA (*defiantly nonresistant*): Wring away! What do I care? I knew you'd strike me one day. (HIGGINS, *about to lay hands on her, recoils.*) Aha! That's done you, 'enry 'iggins, it 'as. Now I don't care that—(*she snaps her fingers in his face*) for your bullying and your big talk.

What a fool I was! What a dominated fool!
To think you were the earth and sky.
What a fool I was! What an addle-pated fool!
What a mutton-headed dolt was I!
No, my reverberating friend,
You are not the beginning and the end!

HIGGINS (*wondering at her*): You impudent hussy! There isn't an idea in your head or a word in your mouth that I haven't put there.

ELIZA:

There'll be spring ev'ry year without you.
England still will be here without you.
There'll be fruit on the tree,
And a shore by the sea;
There'll be crumpets and tea
Without you.

Art and music will thrive without you.
Somehow Keats will survive without you.
And there still will be rain
On that plain down in Spain,
Even that will remain
Without you.
I can do
Without you.

You, dear friend, who talk so well,
You can go to Hertford, Hereford and Hampshire!

They can still rule the land without you.
Windsor Castle will stand without you.
And without much ado
We can all muddle through
Without you!

HIGGINS (*fascinated*): You brazen hussy!
ELIZA:

Without your pulling it, the tide comes in,
Without your twirling it, the earth can spin.
Without your pushing them, the clouds roll by.
If they can do without you, ducky, so can I!

I shall not feel alone without you.
I can stand on my own without you.
So go back in your shell,
I can do bloody well
Without . . .

HIGGINS (*triumphantly*):

By George, I really did it!
I did it! I did it!
I said I'd make a woman
And indeed I did!

I knew that I could do it!
I knew it! I knew it!
I said I'd make a woman
And succeed I did!

Eliza, you're magnificent! Five minutes ago you were a
millstone around my neck. Now you're a tower of
strength, a consort battleship! I like you like this!

(ELIZA *stares at him stonily, then turns on her heels
and walks to the door.*)

ELIZA (*quietly at the door*): Good-bye, Professor Higgins. I shall not be seeing you again. (*She goes.*)

(HIGGINS *is thunderstruck. He walks falteringly across the room and looks after her.*)

HIGGINS (*calling for help*): Mother! Mother!

(MRS. HIGGINS *enters.*)

MRS. HIGGINS: What is it, Henry? What has happened?

HIGGINS (*more to himself*): She's gone!

MRS. HIGGINS (*gently*): Of course, dear. What did you expect?

HIGGINS (*bewildered*): What am I to do?

MRS. HIGGINS: Do without, I suppose.

HIGGINS (*with sudden defiance*): And so I shall! If the Higgins oxygen burns up her little lungs, let her seek some stuffiness that suits her. She's an owl sickened by a few days of my sunshine! Very well, let her go! I can do without her! I can do without anybody! I have my own soul! My own spark of divine fire! (*He marches off.*)

MRS. HIGGINS (*applauding*): Bravo, Eliza! (*She smiles.*)

Scene 6

Outside HIGGINS' *house, Wimpole Street.*

Time: Dusk, that afternoon.

At Rise: HIGGINS *enters bellowing with rage.*

HIGGINS: Damn!! Damn!! Damn!! Damn!! (*A sudden terrifying discovery*) I've grown accustomed to her face!

> She almost makes the day begin.
> I've grown accustomed to the tune
> She whistles night and noon.
> Her smiles. Her frowns.
> Her ups, her downs,
> Are second nature to me now;
> Like breathing out and breathing in.

(*Reassuringly*)

I was serenely independent and content before we met;
Surely I could always be that way again—

(*The reassurance fails.*)

and yet

I've grown accustomed to her looks;
Accustomed to her voice:
Accustomed to her face.

(*Bitterly*) Marry Freddy! What an infantile idea! What a heartless, wicked, brainless thing to do! But she'll regret it! She'll regret it. It's doomed before they even take the vow!

I can see her now:
Mrs. Freddy Eynsford-Hill,
In a wretched little flat above a store.
I can see her now:
Not a penny in the till,
And a bill-collector beating at the door.

She'll try to teach the things I taught her,
And end up selling flow'rs instead;
Begging for her bread and water,
While her husband has his breakfast in bed!

(*Fiendishly pleased*)

In a year or so
When she's prematurely gray,
And the blossoms in her cheek has turned to chalk,

She'll come home and lo!
He'll have upped and run away
With a social climbing heiress from New York!

(*Tragically*)

Poor Eliza!
How simply frightful!
How humiliating!

(*Irresistibly*)

How delightful!

(*He walks to his door.*)

How poignant it will be on that inevitable night when
she hammers on my door in tears and rags. Miserable
and lonely, repentant and contrite. Will I let her in or
hurl her to the wolves? Give her kindness, or the treatment she deserves? Will I take her back, or throw the
baggage out?

(*With sudden benevolence*)

I'm a most forgiving man;
The sort who never could,
Ever would,
Take a position and staunchly never budge.
Just a most forgiving man.

(*With sudden vindictiveness*)

But I shall never take her back,
If she were crawling on her knees.
Let her promise to atone!
Let her shiver, let her moan!
I will slam the door and let the hell-cat freeze!

Marry Freddy! Ha!

(*He takes out his keys to open the door but stops in
despair.*)

But I'm so used to hear her say:
Good morning every day.
Her joys, her woes,
Her highs, her lows
Are second nature to me now;
Like breathing out and breathing in.
I'm very grateful she's a woman
And so easy to forget;
Rather like a habit
One can always break—and yet
I've grown accustomed to the trace
Of something in the air;
Accustomed to her face.

Scene 7

HIGGINS' *study*.

Time: Immediately following.

At Rise: The blue-gray light of early evening pours in through the window. Only one or two lamps are on.

HIGGINS *walks into the room. He walks around thoughtfully. He comes to the xylophone and picks up the mallet and looks at it for a moment. He slowly walks over to the machine by the door and turns it on.* ELIZA's *voice is heard on the speaker. He goes back to his desk and decides to sit on the stool rather than his own chair behind the desk. His hat still on, his head bowed, he listens to the recording.*

ELIZA'S VOICE: I want to be a lady in a flower shop instead of selling flowers at the corner of Tottenham Court Road. But they won't take me unless I talk more genteel. He said he could teach me. Well, here I am ready to pay, not asking any favor—and he treats me as if I was dirt. I know what lessons cost, and I'm ready to pay.

(ELIZA *walks softly into the room and stands for a moment by the machine looking at* HIGGINS.)

HIGGINS' VOICE: It's almost irresistible. She's so deliciously low, so horribly dirty. (ELIZA *turns off the machine.*)

ELIZA (*gently*): I washed my face and hands before I come, I did.

(HIGGINS *straightens up. If he could but let himself, his face would radiate unmistakable relief and joy. If he could but let himself, he would run to her. Instead, he leans back with a contented sigh, pushing his hat forward till it almost covers his face.*)

HIGGINS (*softly*): Eliza? Where the devil are my slippers?

(*There are tears in* ELIZA's *eyes. She understands.*)

The curtain falls slowly

The World's Best Drama

Four Major Plays by Ibsen: Volume One
Translated with a Foreword by Rolf Fjelde
Includes *A Doll House*, *The Wild Duck*,
Hedda Gabler, and *The Master Builder*

Four Major Plays by Ibsen: Volume Two
Translated by Rolf Fjelde with an Afterword by Terry Otten
Includes *Ghosts*, *An Enemy of the People*,
The Lady from the Sea, and *John Gabriel Bookman*

Four Plays by Eugene O'Neill
Introduction by A. R. Gurney
Includes *Anna Christie*, *The Hairy Ape*,
The Emperor Jones, and *Beyond the Horizon*

OUTSTANDING EUROPEAN WORKS

A PORTRAIT OF THE ARTIST AS A YOUNG MAN

by James Joyce

with an Introduction by Langdon Hammer

A masterpiece of subjectivity, a fictionalized memoir, a coming-of-age prose-poem, this brilliant novella introduces Joyce's alter ego, Stephen Daedelus, the hero of *Ulysses*, and begins the narrative experimentation that would help change the concept of literary narrative forever.

DUBLINERS

by James Joyce with an Introduction by Edna O'Brien

In these masterful stories, steeped in realism, Joyce creates an exacting portrait of his native city, showing how it reflects the general decline of Irish culture and civilization. Joyce compels attention by the power of its unique vision of the world, its controlling sense of the truths of human experience.

SILAS MARNER

by George Eliot

with an Introduction by Frederick R. Karl

Eliot's touching novel of a miser and a little child combines the charm of a fairy tale with the humor and pathos of realistic fiction. The gentle linen weaver, Silas Marner, exiles himself to the town of Raveloe after being falsely accused of a heinous theft. There he begins to find redemption and spiritual rebirth through his unselfish love for an abandoned child he discovers in his isolated cottage.

Available wherever books are sold or at

signetclassics.com

READ THE TOP 20
SIGNET CLASSICS

ANIMAL FARM BY GEORGE ORWELL

1984 BY GEORGE ORWELL

NARRATIVE OF THE LIFE OF FREDERICK DOUGLASS
   BY FREDERICK DOUGLASS

BEOWULF (BURTON RAFFEL, TRANSLATOR)

FRANKENSTEIN BY MARY SHELLEY

ALICE'S ADVENTURES IN WONDERLAND &
   THROUGH THE LOOKING GLASS BY LEWIS CARROLL

THE INFERNO BY DANTE

COMMON SENSE, RIGHTS OF MAN, AND OTHER
   ESSENTIAL WRITINGS BY THOMAS PAINE

HAMLET BY WILLIAM SHAKESPEARE

A TALE OF TWO CITIES BY CHARLES DICKENS

THE HUNCHBACK OF NOTRE DAME BY VICTOR HUGO

THE FEDERALIST PAPERS BY ALEXANDER HAMILTON

THE SCARLET LETTER BY NATHANIEL HAWTHORNE

DRACULA BY BRAM STOKER

THE HOUND OF THE BASKERVILLES
   BY SIR ARTHUR CONAN DOYLE

WUTHERING HEIGHTS BY EMILY BRONTË

THE ODYSSEY BY HOMER

A MIDSUMMER NIGHT'S DREAM BY WILLIAM SHAKESPEARE

FRANKENSTEIN; DRACULA; DR. JEKYLL AND MR. HYDE
   BY MARY SHELLEY, BRAM STOKER, AND ROBERT LOUIS STEVENSON

THE CLASSIC SLAVE NARRATIVES
   EDITED BY HENRY LOUIS GATES, JR.